How to Find out about zoo animals

How to

Find out about zoo animals

Barrington Barber and John Eason

STUDIO VISTA London

VNR **VAN NOSTRAND REINHOLD COMPANY** New York

A Studio Vista/Van Nostrand Reinhold How-to Book

Photoset, printed and bound in England by
BAS Printers Limited, Wallop, Hampshire

Published in Great Britain by
Studio Vista
Blue Star House, Highgate Hill, London N19
and in the United States by
Van Nostrand Reinhold Company
A Division of Litton Educational Publishing, Inc.
450 West 33rd Street, New York, N.Y. 10001

Library of Congress Catalog Card Number 70 39849
ISBN 0 289 70244 5

Contents

Introduction

Why do tigers have stripes? Why does the lemur have large eyes? Why does an eagle have a hooked beak? You will soon find out the answers to these questions and many more when you read this book. There are animal models and masks, skeletons and gliding birds to make as well as puzzles and quizzes to pit your wits against.

Next time you visit the zoo or a natural history museum you will astound your friends by the amount you already know about zoo animals.

Help! What is it?

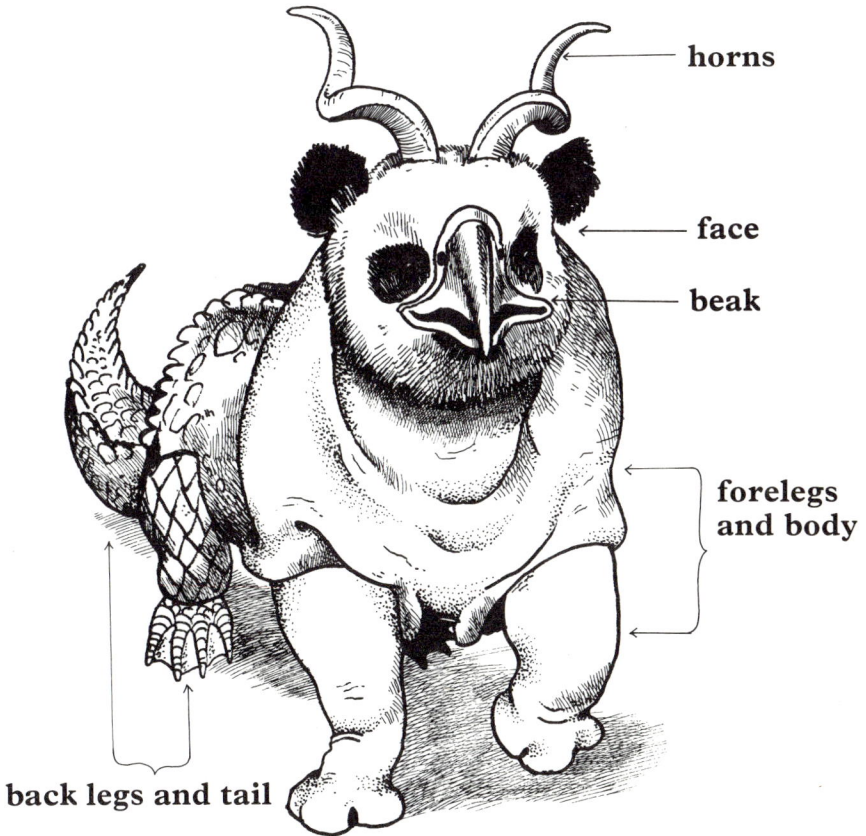

horns

face

beak

forelegs
and body

back legs and tail

If you saw *this* animal advancing towards you—even
from behind the bars of a cage—it would be very
understandable if you just turned and ran. But don't
worry; there is no such creature. It is a composite
animal made up of the parts of others. Can you guess
from which animals they come? (Answers on page 64)

Now make up your own monster from the parts of
other animals.

Armour-plated animals

Armadillo
Some animals are well protected from their enemies by armour plating, like the armadillo. To make a model armadillo, stuff an old grey sock firmly with rags and tie each end with thread to make the head and tail. Cover the body with old beads stitched in position. Use pieces of felt for ears, buttons for eyes. Glue on cardboard legs and feet.

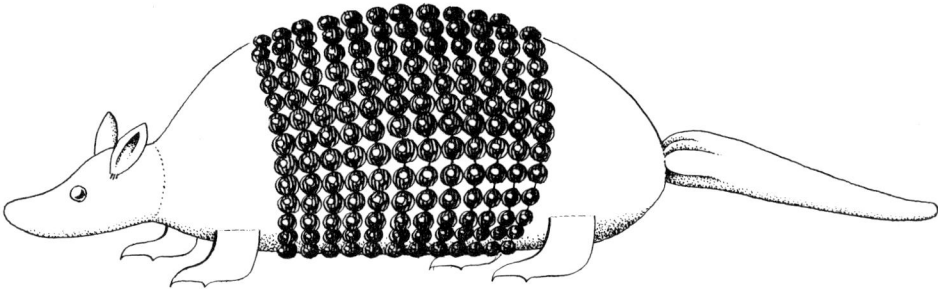

Snail

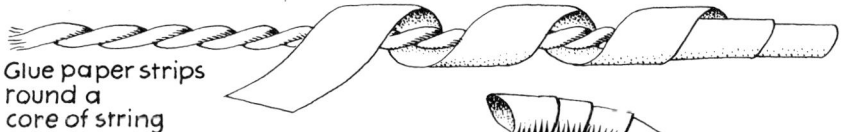

Glue paper strips
round a
core of string

Glue strips of paper round a core of fairly thick string. When the glue is dry, twist and glue the string into a coil. Paint the shell yellow with brown markings.

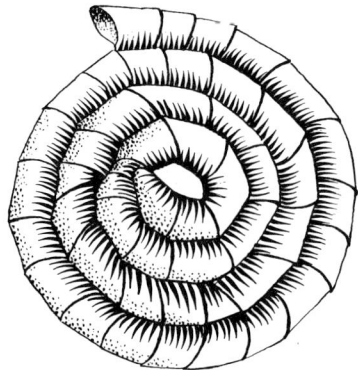

8

Crocodile

Model a crocodile in Plasticine or another modelling material. Make his armour-plating by covering his body with broken nut shells. Use glass beads for the eyes and strong rose thorns for the teeth.

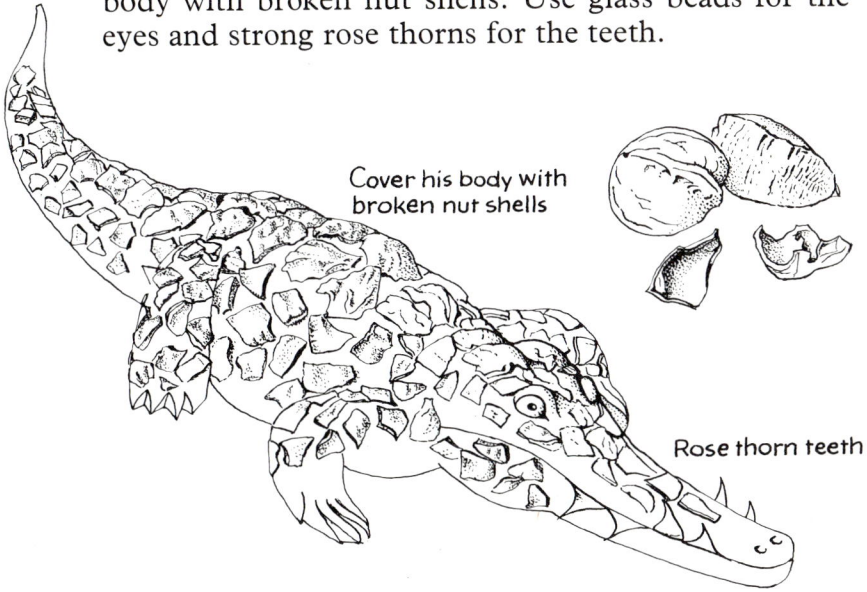

Cover his body with broken nut shells

Rose thorn teeth

Hedgehog

Make in the same way as the crocodile but try to find something really prickly for the spines. Burs or sweet chestnut spines are ideal.

Follow this drawing to make the Plasticine body

Cover with sweet chestnut spines

Tortoise

To make a tortoise you need another stuffed sock. Cut the fingers off an old glove to make the legs and head. Stuff them with cotton wool and sew them to the body. Glue walnut shells to the sock to make the shell and sew on buttons for the eyes.

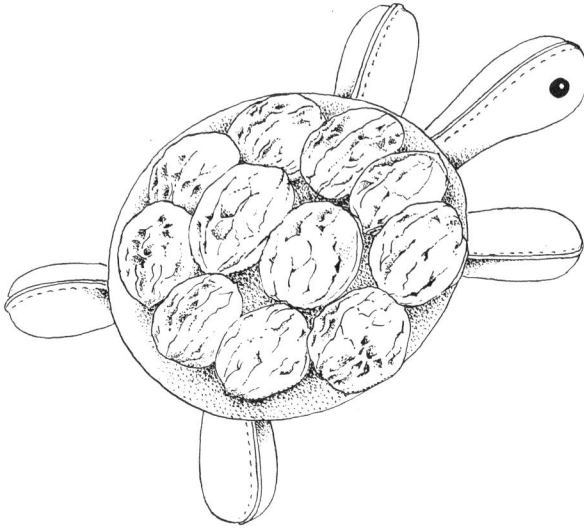

Spiny anteater

Make an Australian spiny anteater in the same way as the hedgehog, but use shortened toothpicks or cocktail sticks for his long strong spines.

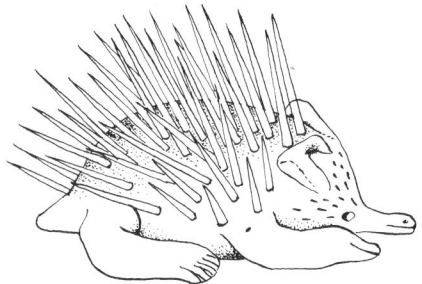

Porcupine
Pine needles make very good porcupine spines.

Follow this drawing to help you make his Plasticine body

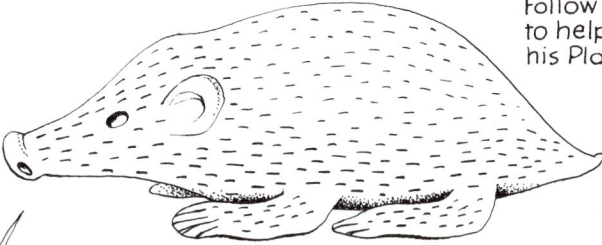

Make holes in the Plasticine with a pencil point and place a double pine needle like this in each hole

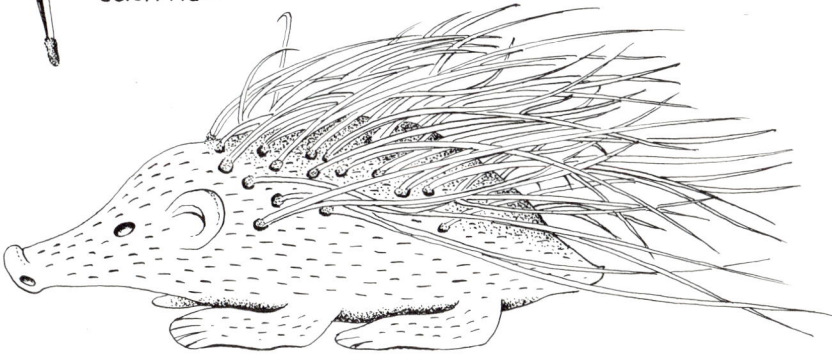

What other kinds of armour-plated animals can you think of? (See page 64)

Feet and claws

Here are some animals without legs and some legs without bodies. Can you match them up correctly? Draw the bodies and legs onto thin card, cut them out and pin them together with brass paper fasteners to make animals with movable legs.

Answers on page 64.

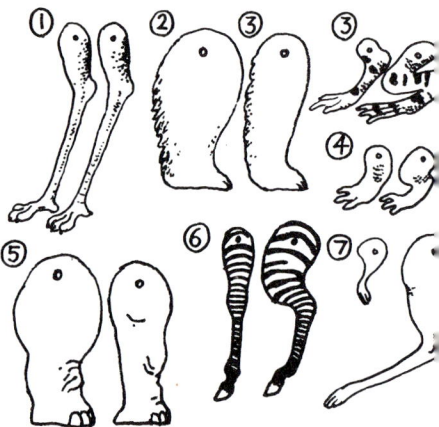

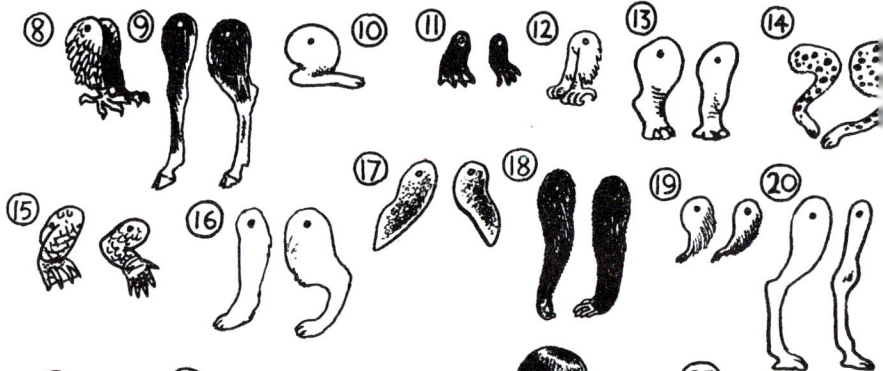

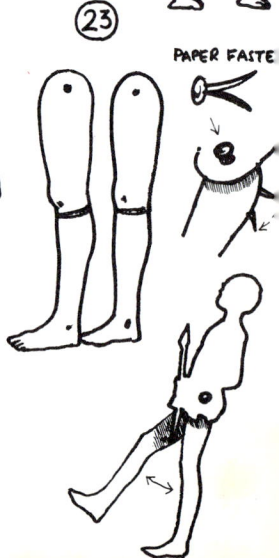

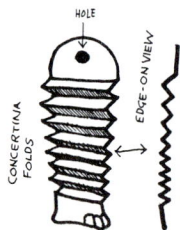

PAPER FASTE

CONCERTINA FOLDS

HOLE

EDGE-ON VIEW

BOUNCE BOUNCE

FOR FUN...
ALTERNATIVE
LEGS FOR THE
ELEPHANT!

Bills and beaks

Birds have different beaks according to the kind of food they eat. Can you link these birds with their beaks? Trace a bird and then trace onto it the beak you think fits best. (Answers page 64)

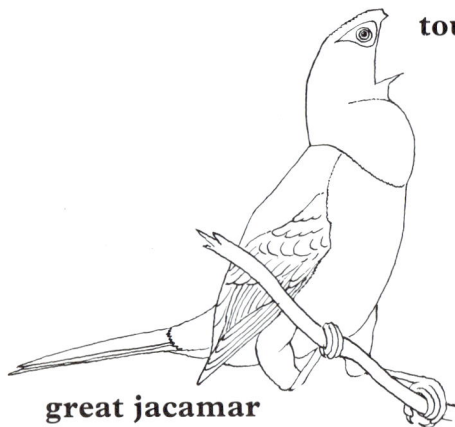

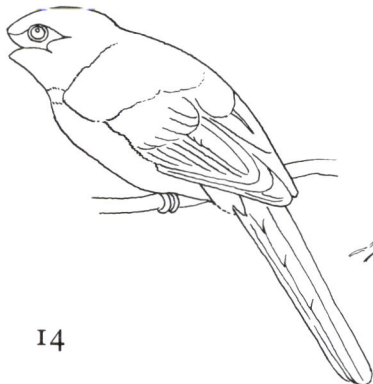

What kind of a bill do these birds have?

a an insect eating-bird
b a seed-eating bird
c a fruit-eating bird
d a flesh-eating bird

Give an example of each of these kinds of bird. (Answers page 64)

toucan

bullfinch

great jacamar

gannet

bald eagle  **limpkin**

oropendola

 **cockatoo**

ory-billed woodpecker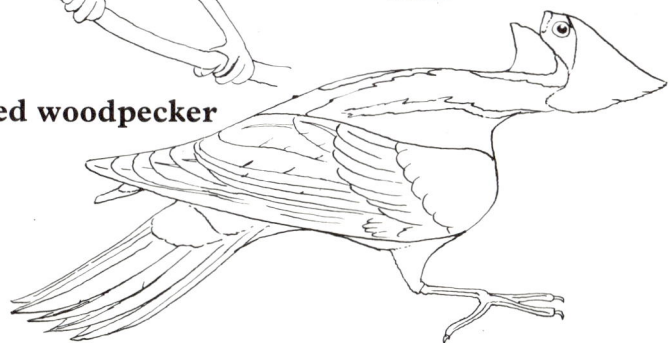

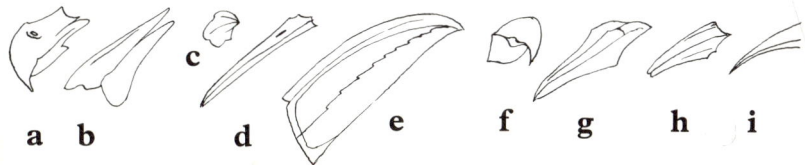

a b   c   d   e   f g h i

Habitats

A habitat is the natural home of an animal, the area where it is born and grows up. Try to link up the animals and birds on this page with the six different habitats on page 17 and the mountain habitat on page 19. Make notes when you go to the zoo or use animal encyclopaedias to find out what you want to know.

(Answers page 64)

Loris Hippo Cheetah Zebra Water-storing tortoise Addax antelope Albatross Lynx

Leopard Flamingo Springbok Tapir Moose Waterbuck Boobie Chamois

Giraffe Water buffalo Orang-utan Gecko Komodo dragon Mink Spoonbill Seal

Shoebill Crocodile Sand fox Long-eared owl Okapi Tiger Land rail Alpine Ibex

Stone Curlew Lion Yak Gannet Gibbon Rhino Pelican Puma

Blue hare Wildebeeste Mountain vulture Spotted linsang Baboon Golden eagle Silver pheasant Vulture

Toucan Beaver Stork Pine marten Bighorn ram Antelope Vicuna Brown bear

1 Inland waters

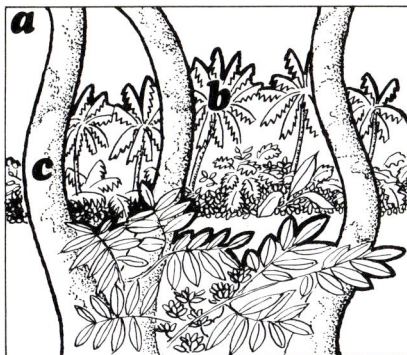

2 Tropical forest

3 Tropical grassland

4 Coniferous (evergreen) forest

5 Oceans and islands

6 Desert

17

Make a 3-D model habitat

You need: three pieces of stiff paper or thin card, one about 38 × 28 cm. (15 × 11 in.) and two about 28 × 15 cm. (11 × 6 in.); paints or crayons; scissors.

The model shown here is of a mountain and forest habitat, but you could make one of any of the habitats on page 17. The letters **a**, **b** and **c** are marked on each drawing to help you decide what to draw on each piece of card.

Fold the largest piece of card across the middle to divide the background from the foreground. Make a strut (see diagram **a**) to help the background stand up.

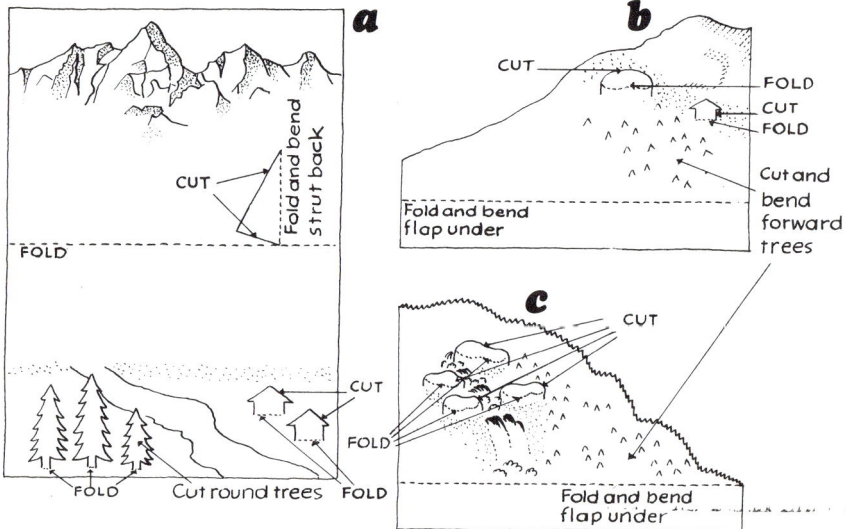

Draw the outlines of mountains onto the background and a stream, trees and buildings on the foreground. Cut round the sides and tops of the trees and buildings but not along the bottoms. Fold them forwards to make them stand up.

Cut wavy skylines on the other two pieces of card (**b** and **c**). Draw onto them the outlines of rocks, boulders and treetops. Cut round the sides and top of each and bend them slightly forwards. Bend back a flap along the bottom of pieces **b** and **c** and glue them onto the foreground.

Paint or crayon the whole model. Now copy and cut out some of the animals and birds on page 16 and glue them in position on the model.

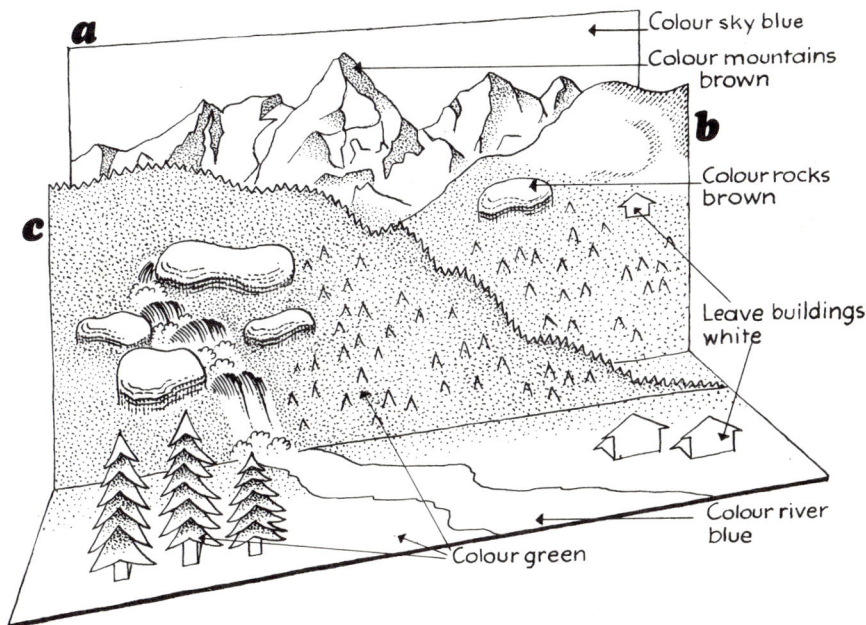

Colour sky blue
Colour mountains brown
Colour rocks brown
Leave buildings white
Colour river blue
Colour green

Africa

This vast continent, teeming with animal life, supplies the zoos of the world with many splendid species of wild animals.

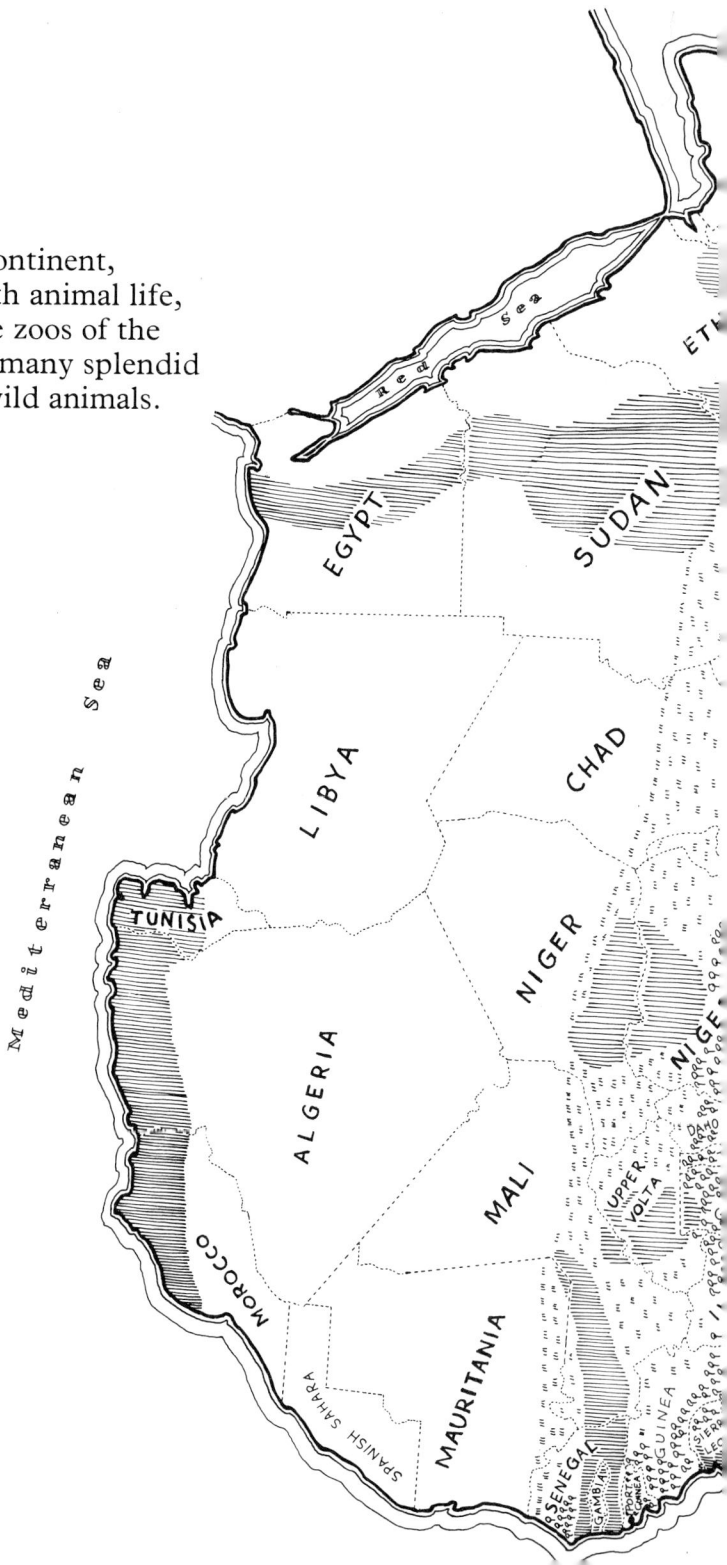

Mediterranean Sea

Red Sea

EGYPT

SUDAN

ETH

LIBYA

CHAD

TUNISIA

NIGER

NIGE

ALGERIA

MALI

UPPER VOLTA

MOROCCO

MAURITANIA

SPANISH SAHARA

GUINEA

SENEGAL

GAMBIA

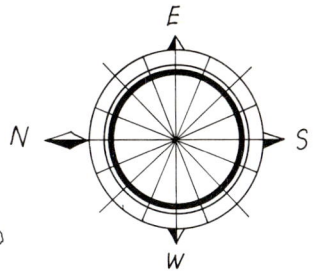

Indian Ocean

MADAGASCAR

E

N   S

W

KENYA

MOZAMBIQUE

TANZANIA

GANDA

CONGO

ANGOLA

ZAMBIA

RHODESIA

BOTSWANA
LAND

SOUTH
AFRICA

SOUTH WEST AFRICA

CONGO

GABON

Atlantic Ocean

forest

grassland

desert

**cultivated
areas**

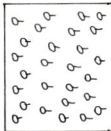

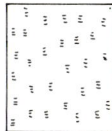

21

African animals
How many members of the ape family can you find?
(Answers page 65)

CHEETAH

ZEBRA

OSTRICH

GIRAFFE

ELEPHANT

IMPALA	ELAND	 SUNI	KUDU	WILDEBEESTE (GNU) 

GRANT'S GAZELLE	SABLE ANTELOPE	WATERBUCK	HARTEBEESTE	KLIPSPRINGER

BLACK RHINO	WHITE RHINO	BUFFALO	WARTHOG	GOSHAWK

HAMADRYAS	CHACMA BABOON	LION	GROUND HORNBILL	CAPE HUNTING DOG

VERVET MONKEY	CROWNED CRANE	HYENA	JACKAL	PUFF-ADDER

LEOPARD	EGYPTIAN VULTURE	LAPPET-FACED VULTURE	MARABOU	MEERKAT

AARDVARK	HYRAX	TAWNY EAGLE	SCORPION	GORILLA

American animals
Which of these animals are reptiles?
(Answers page 65)

BISON

PRAIRIE CHICKEN

SKUNK

PRAIRIE DOG

MULE DEER

GOPHER

MOOSE

GOLDEN EAGLE

COYOTE

VISCACHA

MUSK - OX

WOLF

WHITE-TAILED DEER

PAMPA DEER

RHEA

PAMPAS GUINEA PIG

CONDOR

GIANT ANTEATER

PAMPA FOX

FAIRY ARMADILLO

RATTLESNAKE

TOUCAN

ARMADILLO

PORCUPINE

CARIBOU

VAMPIRE BAT

SPIDER MONKEY

VICUNA

CALIFORNIAN SEA LION

GRIZZLY BEAR

CAPUCHIN MONKEY

THREE-TOED SLOTH

PUMA

MARMOSET

PECCARY

JAGUAR

BOA CONSTRICTOR

HUMMING BIRD

IGUANA

BEAVER

North America

Many North American varieties of animal life are similar to those in Europe and Asia.

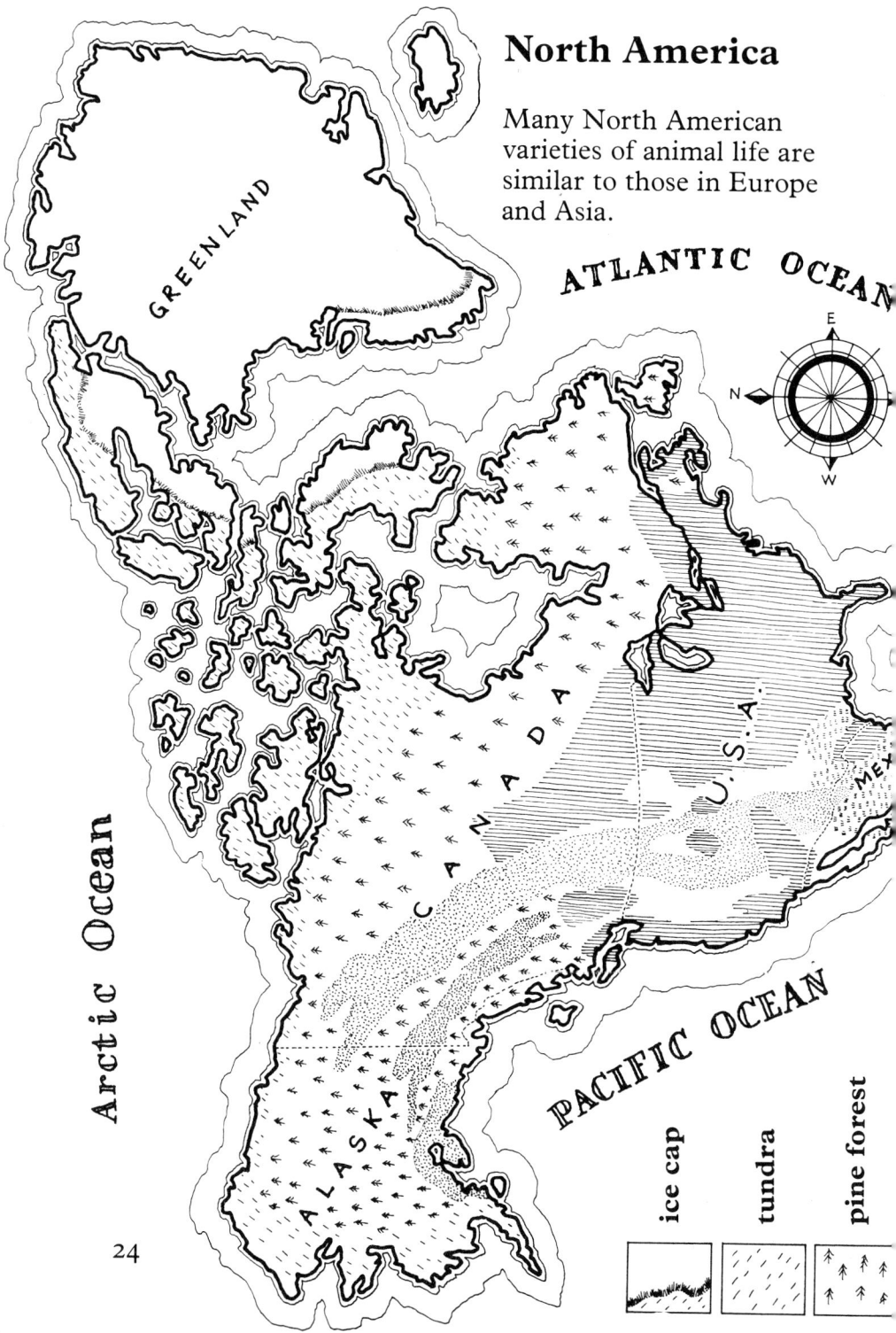

ATLANTIC OCEAN

GREENLAND

Arctic Ocean

CANADA

U.S.A.

MEX.

ALASKA

PACIFIC OCEAN

ice cap   **tundra**   **pine forest**

 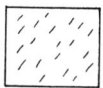

24

South America

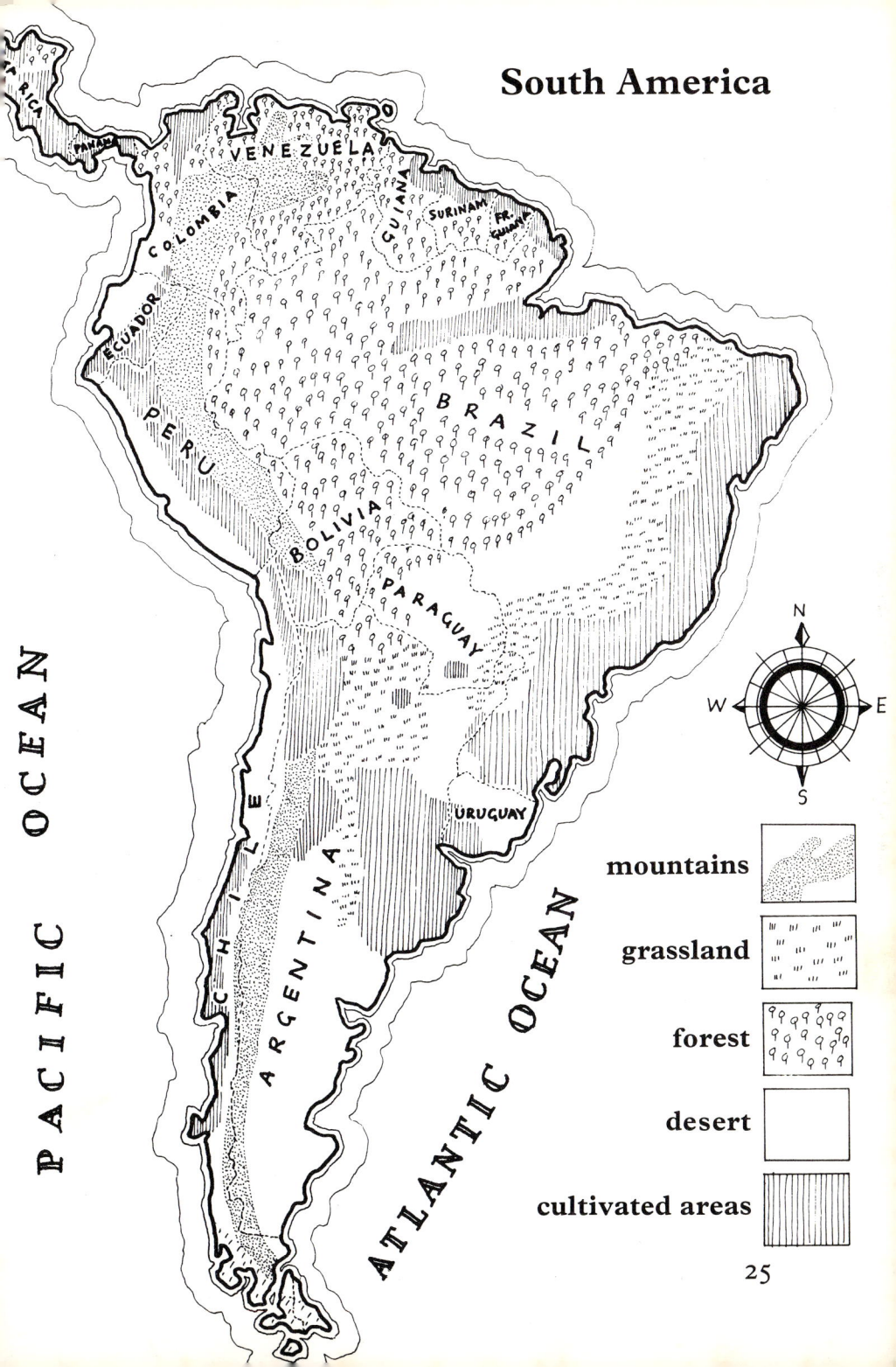

PACIFIC OCEAN

ATLANTIC OCEAN

COSTA RICA
PANAMA
VENEZUELA
COLOMBIA
GUIANA
SURINAM
FR. GUIANA
ECUADOR
PERU
BRAZIL
BOLIVIA
PARAGUAY
CHILE
ARGENTINA
URUGUAY

N
W — E
S

mountains
grassland
forest
desert
cultivated areas

25

Asia

The ancient world, home
of many strange animals.

 desert

 grassland

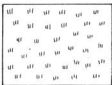 forest

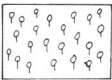 pine forest

 mountains

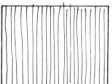 cultivated areas

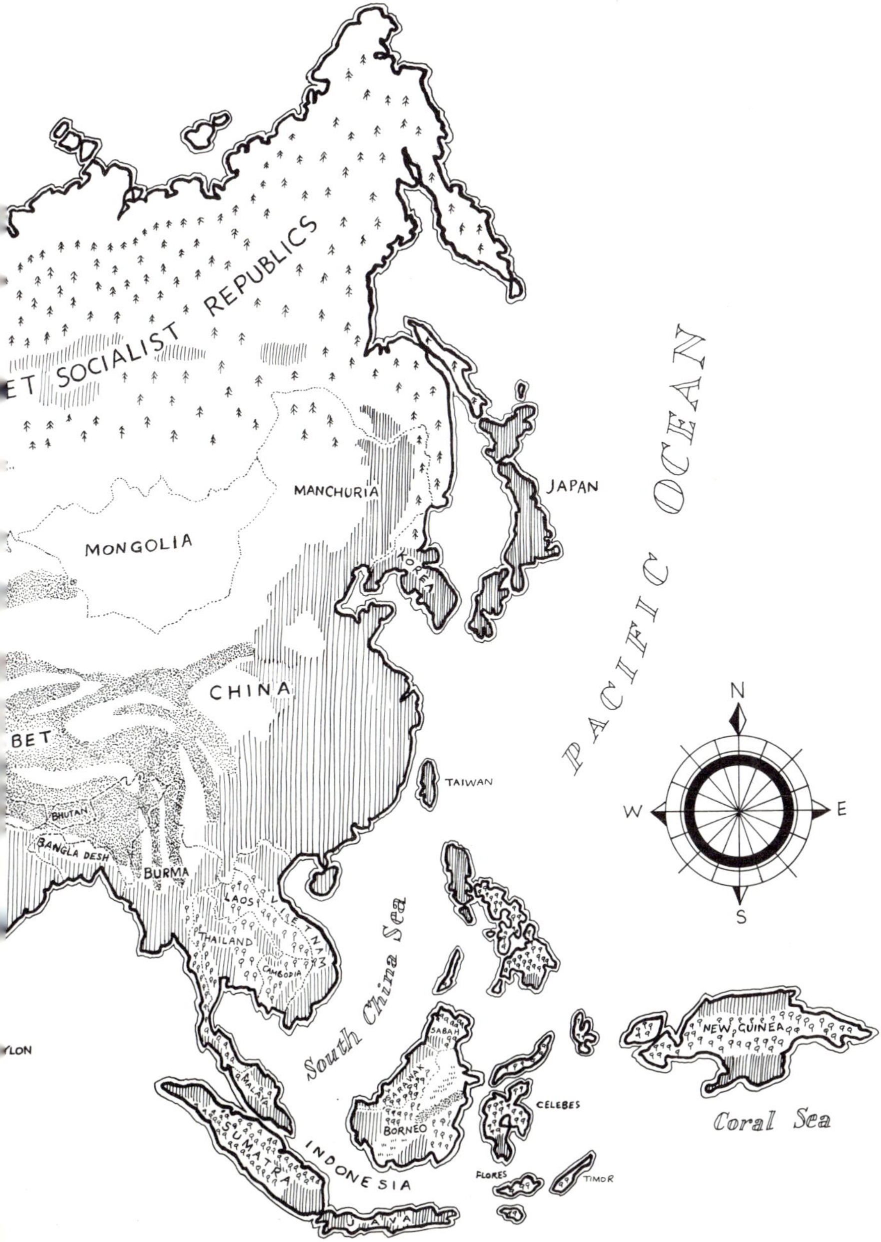

ET SOCIALIST REPUBLICS
MANCHURIA
MONGOLIA
JAPAN
KOREA
PACIFIC OCEAN
CHINA
BET
TAIWAN
N
W
E
S
BHUTAN
BANGLA DESH
BURMA
LAOS
VIETNAM
THAILAND
CAMBODIA
South China Sea
YLON
SABAH
SARAWAK
BORNEO
NEW GUINEA
CELEBES
Coral Sea
MALAYA
SUMATRA
INDONESIA
FLORES
TIMOR
JAVA

Asian animals
Which of these animals eat insects? (Answers page 65)

INDIAN ELEPHANT	TIGER	DROMEDARY	GIANT PANDA	KING COBRA	MONGOOSE

BLACKBUCK	BACTRIAN CAMEL	POLAR BEAR	ARCTIC FOX	LEMMING	SIKA DEER

REINDEER	WOLF	BROWN BEAR	LYNX	WEASEL	OSPREY

ROE DEER	RED DEER	RED FOX	WILD BOAR	SCORPION	HIMALAYAN BLACK BEAR

CHINESE MUNTJAC	JAPANESE MACAQUE	TAWNY EAGLE	WILD ASS	PANGOLIN	GIANT CRANE

Australian animals
Which of these mammals lay eggs? (Answers page 65)

KOOKABURRA	KANGAROO	PLATYPUS	WALLABY	KOALA BEAR	TASMANIAN DEVIL

SHEEP	WOMBAT	SUGAR GLIDER	BANDICOOT	NUMBAT	LYRE BIRD

EMU	RABBIT	FROGMOUTH	QUOKKA	SPINY ANTEATER	GOANNA

Australia

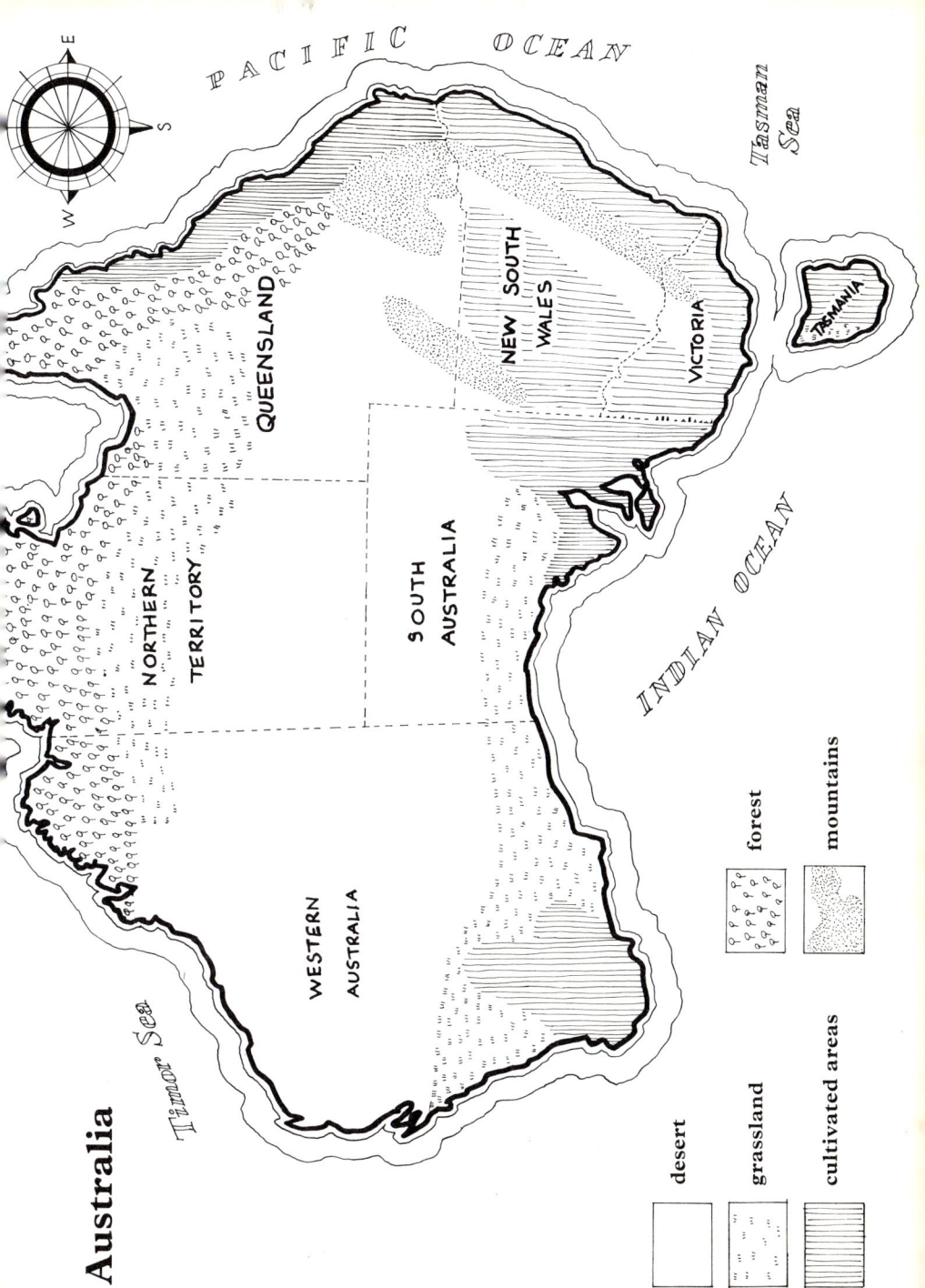

PACIFIC OCEAN

Tasman Sea

Timor Sea

INDIAN OCEAN

QUEENSLAND

NEW SOUTH WALES

VICTORIA

TASMANIA

NORTHERN TERRITORY

SOUTH AUSTRALIA

WESTERN AUSTRALIA

desert

grassland

cultivated areas

forest

mountains

The MATCHBOX ZOO

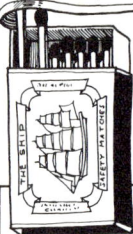

VISIT THE ZOO AND DRAW, OR COLLECT PAMPHLETS AND CARDS SHOWING AS MANY ANIMAL PICTURES AS POSSIBLE.

THEN COLLECT LOTS OF MATCHBOXES, CHEESEBOXES, CIGARETTE PACKETS, KITCHEN-SIZE MATCHBOXES, CHOCOLATE BOXES, ETC. AND SOME THIN CARD, GLUE, STICKY-TAPE, BOTTLETOPS AND CORKS.

① FIRST OF ALL MAKE SURE THAT YOUR ANIMAL PICTURES WILL FIT INTO MATCHBOXES. THE BIGGER ONES CAN GO INTO CIGARETTE PACKS OR KITCHEN MATCHBOXES.

② YOU WILL ALSO NEED A SHARP BLADE — THERE ARE PLENTY OF SPECIAL CARD-CUTTING KNIVES SOLD AT DRAWING OFFICE SUPPLIERS. — OR A RAZOR BLADE BROKEN IN HALF... THUS!

③ NOW CUT OUT SLOTS IN ONE OF THE OUTER PART OF A MATCHBOX...

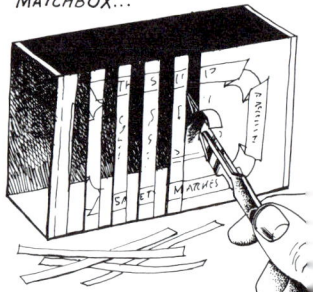

④ PAINT THE SIDES AND BACK IN INTERESTING SOLID COLOURS, THEN WRITE NAMES ON SELF-ADHESIVE LABELS WITH COLOURED PENCILS.

LION

⑤ THEN CUT BARS IN THE ENDS OF THE TRAY PART OF THE BOX. PAINT THE INSIDE BLACK OR A CONTRASTING COLOUR TO THE ANIMAL.

⑥ GLUE A PICTURE OF AN ANIMAL ON TO A PIECE OF THIN CARD, AND CUT IT OUT LEAVING AN EXTRA PIECE OF BASE ALONG THE BOTTOM WHICH YOU THEN FOLD BACK.

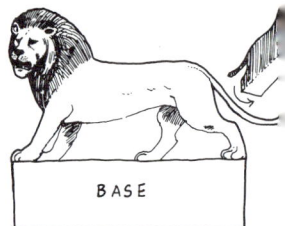

BASE

⑦ NOW GLUE THE ANIMAL INTO THE BOX ——— AND SLIDE THE TRAY INTO PLACE. THEN MOUNT THE WHOLE THING ONTO THE UP-TURNED TRAY OF ANOTHER BOX.

NOW REPEAT THE EXERCISE WITH OTHER ANIMALS UNTIL YOU HAVE MADE A GOOD NUMBER OF CAGES.

⑧ GLUE SOME CAGES BACK TO BACK AND IN ROWS TO MAKE A COMPLEX OF CAGES ONE SPECIES — AS SHOWN.

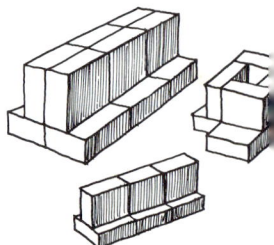

9 TO MAKE A PENGUIN POOL TAKE A LARGE CHOCOLATE-BOX OR SIMILAR CARTON...

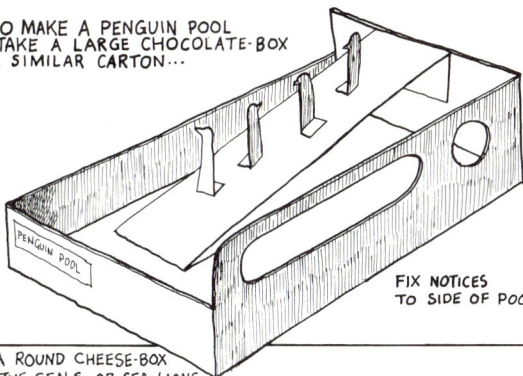

CUT SIDES AS SHOWN AND PAINT INSIDE OF BOX LIGHT BLUE OR TURQUOISE. PAINT OUTSIDE PALE GREY. FIX IN SLOPE OF WHITE CARD WITH PENGUINS ATTACHED.

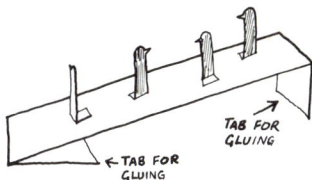

PENGUIN POOL

FIX NOTICES TO SIDE OF POOL

TAB FOR GLUING

← TAB FOR GLUING

USE A ROUND CHEESE-BOX FOR THE SEALS OR SEA-LIONS. PAINT THE INSIDE A GREY-GREEN AND GLUE DIFFERENT BOTTLE-TOPS OR CORKS IN THE CENTRE AS ROCKS FOR THE SEALS TO BASK ON. PAINT THESE GREY-BROWN. FIX ONE SEAL ONTO THE ROCKS AND ANOTHER HALF-SEAL IN THE POOL TO LOOK AS IF IT IS SWIMMING. PAINT WAVE MARKS TO SHOW THAT IT IS MOVING.

ROCKS CAN ALSO BE MADE BY USING SMOOTH PEBBLES AND GLUING THEM DOWN OR FIXING THEM TOGETHER WITH PLASTICINE

FOR THE ELEPHANT-HOUSE FIX THREE LARGE MATCHBOXES (KITCHEN-SIZE) TOGETHER, AS SHOWN ABOVE, WITH STICKY TAPE. A LARGE DOOR IN ONE SIDE.

12

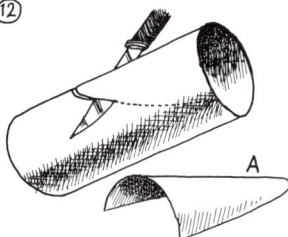

CUT A PIECE OFF A CYLINDRICAL PACK— SCOURING POWDERS ARE OFTEN PACKED LIKE THIS. YOU SHOULD END UP WITH A SHAPE LIKE "A" ABOVE.

A

13 THEN FIX IT AS A ROOF ONTO THE THREE BOXES. STICKY TAPE WORKS BEST WITH ODD SHAPES, OR ELSE BALSA CEMENT.

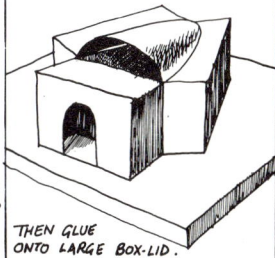

THEN GLUE ONTO LARGE BOX-LID.

PAINT THE STAND GREEN AND SAND-COLOURED AND PLACE ELEPHANTS IN THE ENTRANCE AND AROUND IT. IF YOU CAN FIND A PICTURE OF A BABY ELEPHANT, PUT HIM WITH A KEEPER.

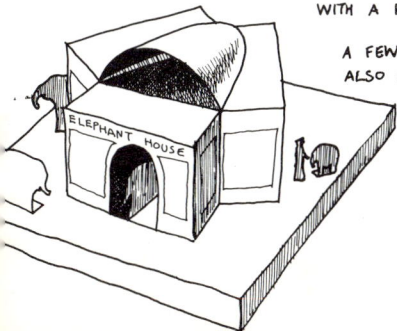

A FEW TREES MAY ALSO COME IN HANDY HERE.

ELEPHANT HOUSE

ALMOST ANY LARGE, RATHER ODD-SHAPED CONSTRUCTION WOULD MAKE A GOOD ELEPHANT-HOUSE AND IT WOULD BE WORTHWHILE EXPERIMENTING.

JUST REMEMBER THAT ELEPHANTS NEED BARN-LIKE QUARTERS WITH LARGE AIRY OPENINGS.

MORE OVER THE PAGE...

(15)

TREES CAN BE MADE BY CUTTING OUT PICTURES OF THEM, MOUNTING THEM ON CARD AND MAKING A FOLD-UP BASE.

A STRUT CAN BE FIXED ON TO THE BACK TO MAKE THE TRUNK MORE RIGID. MAKE A GOOD FEW OF THESE.

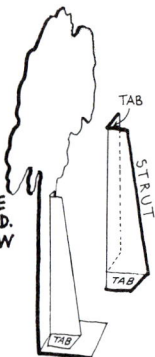

TAB

STRUT

TAB

TAB

ANOTHER WAY IS BY USING TW STUCK INTO CORKS. THEN DIP A PIECE OF FOAM SPONGE INTO GREEN PAINT AND PUSH IT ONTO THE TOP OF THE TWIG. THE CORK BASE CAN BE STUCK DOWN ONTO THE BASE-BOARD TO KEEP THE TREE STEADY.

(16)

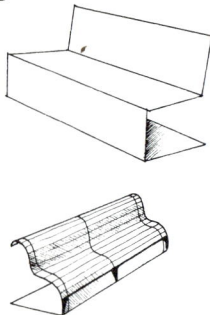

SEATS CAN BE MADE OUT OF FOLDED PAPER — OR JUST BENT PAPER, OR THIN CARD.

THESE CAN THEN BE PAINTED IN GREEN AND BLACK STRIPES.

(17)

NOW ALL YOU NEED IS A LARGE BASE-BOARD MADE OF CARD OR HARDBOARD WHICH YOU PAINT WITH GRASS AND PATHS.

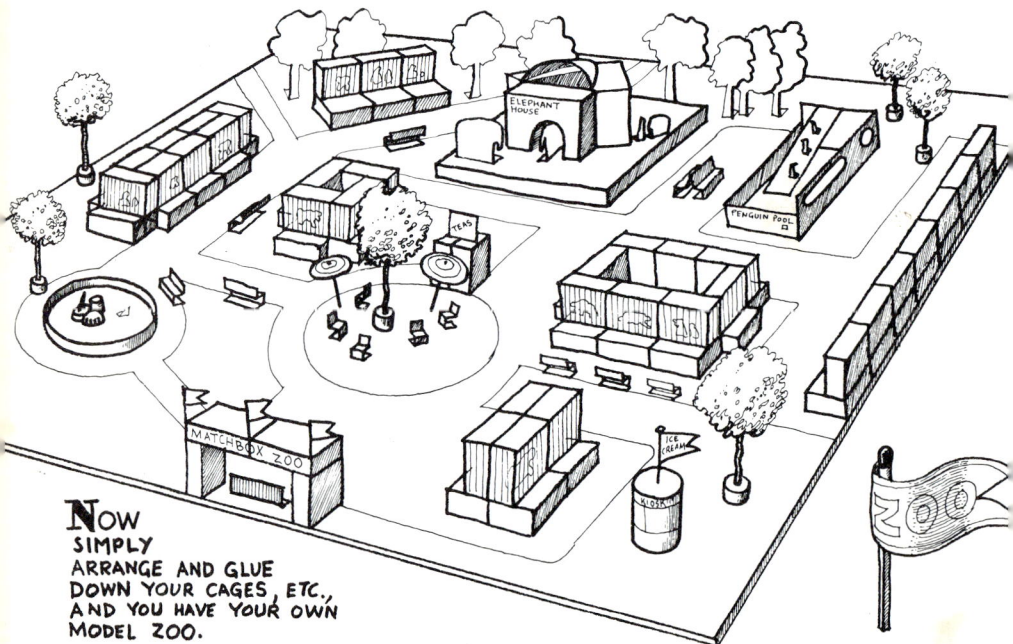

ELEPHANT HOUSE

PENGUIN POOL

TEAS

MATCHBOX ZOO

ICE CREAM

KIOSK

ZOO

NOW SIMPLY ARRANGE AND GLUE DOWN YOUR CAGES, ETC., AND YOU HAVE YOUR OWN MODEL ZOO.

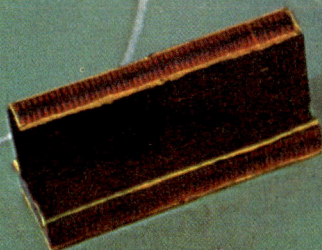

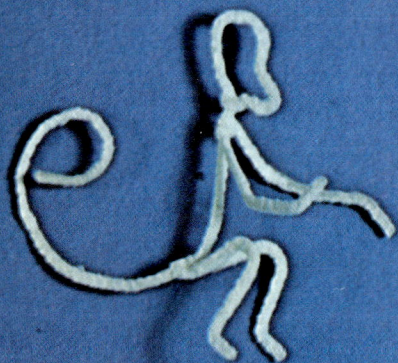

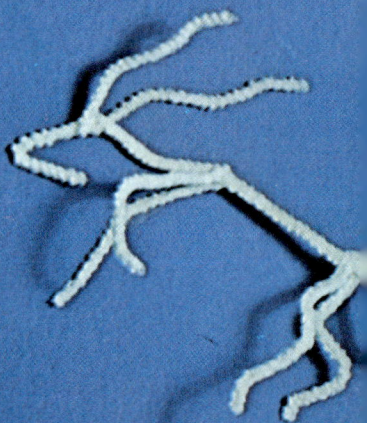

Animal characteristics

Animals can be grouped together in different classes such as hunting animals, grazing, and nocturnal animals. Do you know the main characteristics of each group? You should spot a clue or two while making these models.

1 Hunting animals

Use a narrow cardboard tube for the body of a lion leaping on his prey (see facing page) and a ping-pong ball for the head. Make a mane and tail of thick string frayed at the ends and make legs out of cardboard.

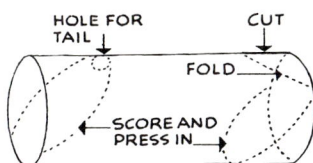

Shape rear end of lion by scoring on dotted line with a knife and pressing in. Then make hole for string tail and glue in the hole

HOLE FOR TAIL

CUT

FOLD

SCORE AND PRESS IN

Cut slit 2 cm. (¾ in) long in from edge and fold back flap on each side for gluing to the head.

Score here and press in to shape chest

2 Grazing animals

Make a zebra with a ping-pong ball for a body and a head, neck and legs of stiff paper.

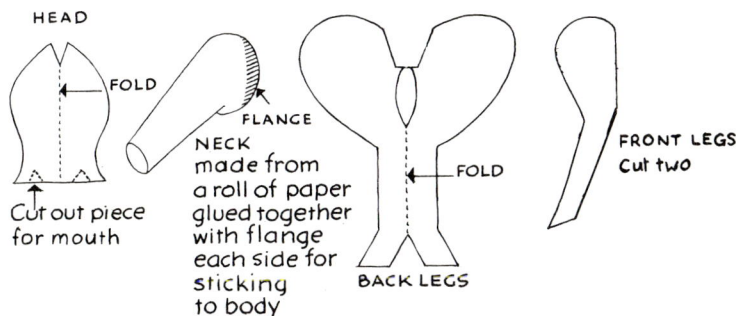

HEAD

FOLD

Cut out piece for mouth

FLANGE

NECK made from a roll of paper glued together with flange each side for sticking to body

FOLD

BACK LEGS

FRONT LEGS Cut two

3 Flesh-eating animals

With a black, felt-tipped pen draw the mouth, eyes and ears of a flesh-eating animal on a ping-pong ball. Think carefully about the kind of teeth it should have. If you wish, you can glue the ball to a shield cut out of cardboard and painted a bright colour. It will then look like the hunting trophies big game hunters used to have.

4 Foraging animals

The monkey on page 34 is made from four pipe-cleaners. You need one for his body and head, another for his tail, and two more for his limbs. Start by bending one pipecleaner to make the head and body and then twist on the legs and arms. Add the tail last. Use the picture as a guide for the shape of the legs, arms and tail.

5 Hunted animals

You can also make a horned antelope from pipe-cleaners (see page 34 once more). You need one for its head, neck and body and an extra piece for its tail. Two more are needed for the legs and another one for the horns. Look at the picture to see where to fix them together and how to bend them into shape.

6 Nocturnal animals

Glue two large dark buttons onto a ping-pong ball to look like the very large eyes of a nocturnal, or night-loving, animal. Draw on a nose and mouth with a black felt-tipped pen. Glue it onto a brightly coloured card-board shield as you did for the flesh-eater. To make a pair of really eye-catching creatures.

Can you answer these questions?
(Answers on page 65)

1 What other classes of animals can you see at the zoo? Name four, and give an example of each.

2 You have made six models, all of animals with different characteristics. Can you say what these characteristics are?

3 Can you name some more examples of:

a) hunting animals
b) grazing animals
c) flesh-eating animals
d) foraging animals
e) hunted animals
f) nocturnal animals

4 Which is the fastest animal in the world?

37

Why are some animals patterned?

Copy this zebra onto a folded sheet of paper. Try to make it about 12 cm. (or 5 in.) across. Cut round the outline, through both thicknesses of paper to make two zebras. Paint one of them plain black and copy the black zebra markings from page 39 onto the other one.

Now lay each one in turn on the zebra markings in this book. Do you see the difference? The patterned zebra is much less noticeable than the other on the patterned background. This is why zebras and other animals that live in areas of tall grassland have stripey patterns. And this is why giraffes and other animals that live among leafy trees have patchy markings. The markings are called camouflage.

leopard

linsang

Do you know . . . .
. . . which animal's markings are shown opposite?
. . . why some animals
have white bellies?
(Answers page 65)

tiger

clouded leopard

Colour them correctly

Trace these birds and take
the outline drawings with
you to the zoo. Colour in
all the areas with the
correct colours.

**yellow-headed
Amazon parrot**

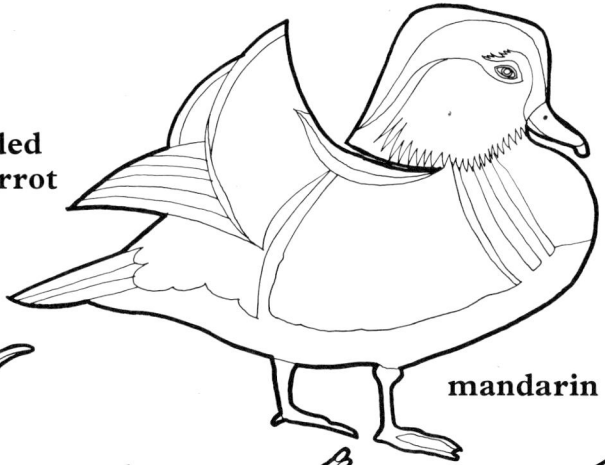

mandarin duck

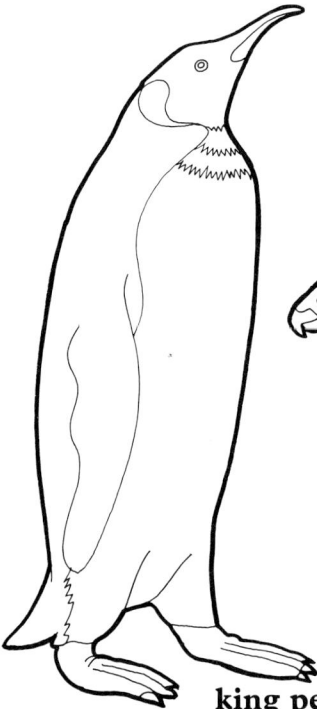

**rainbow
lorikeet**

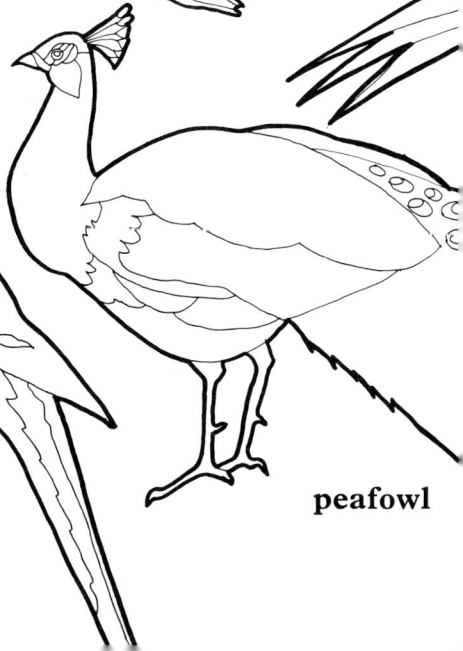

peafowl

king penguin

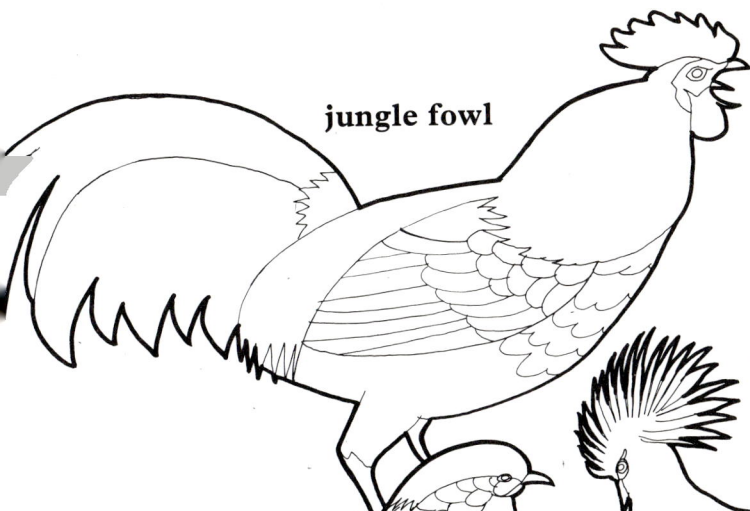

jungle fowl

blue-crowned
pigeon

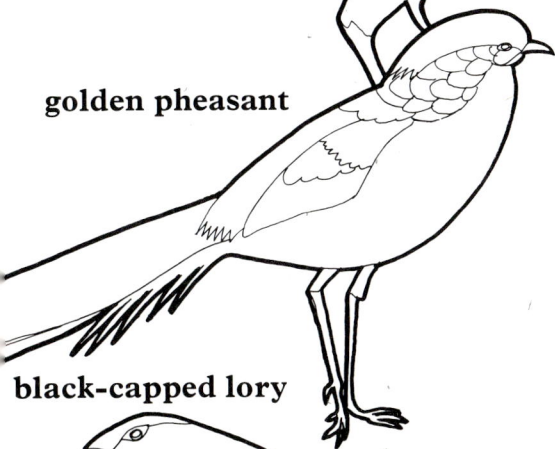

golden pheasant

black-capped lory

golden conure

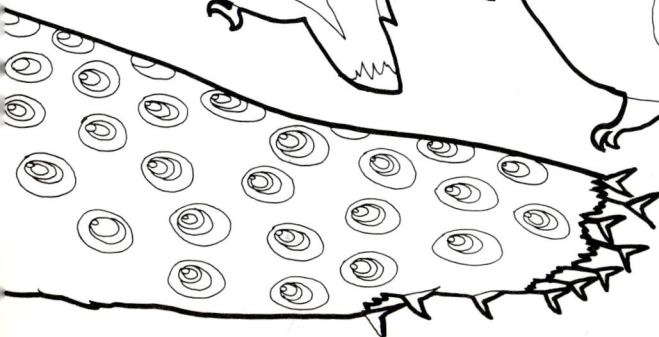

43

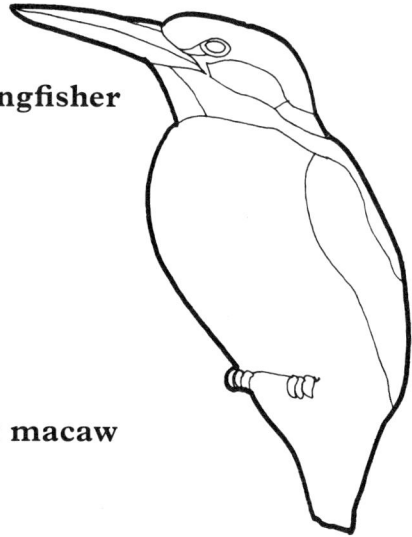

kingfisher

scarlet macaw

blue tit

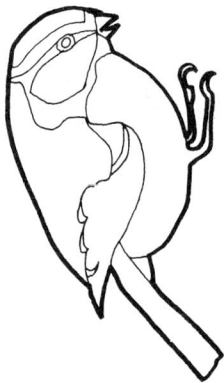

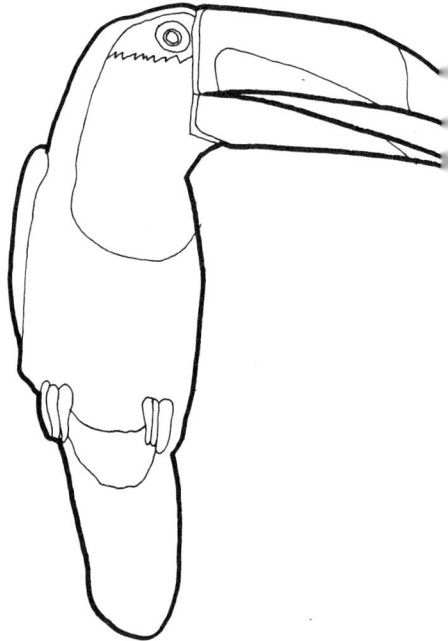

sulphur-breasted toucan

Where do these birds live? (Answers page 66)

Animal crossword

Clues across

1 A wild dog from the Antipodes
3 Sea swallow
5 Fleet-footed, grazing, grassland animal
6 Black and white moorland bird with corny name
10 Fishermen use it
13 Browsing animal like a small rhino
14 Snakes with unusual skill

(Answers page 66)

Clues down

1 Bird with no fine feathers is this
2 A night screamer
3 The black end of an ermine's tail
4 Small water reptile
6 Largest sea mammals
7 No creature can live long if it doesn't do this
8 Large, horned no. 5 across
9 What no. 5 across and no. 8 down are fond of
12 Familar pet with fierce cousins

Gliding birds

Aeroplanes are moved through the air by their engines, while birds rely on their wing beats to get along. Many birds also glide, resting on the air with their wings and tail fully spread. Try making these gliding birds from paper and Balsa wood. They should need only a gentle push to make them 'fly'.

Paper swallow
You need:
A sheet of white drawing paper about 23 cm. (9 in.) square. (You could also try making a larger swallow with thicker paper.)

End view of body

Body is made by folding paper to give four thicknesses

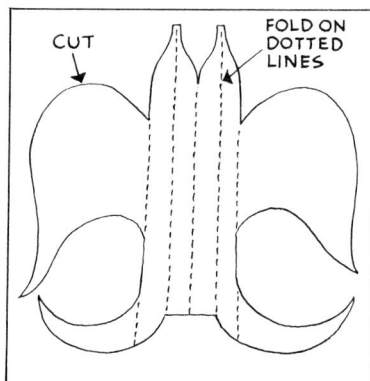

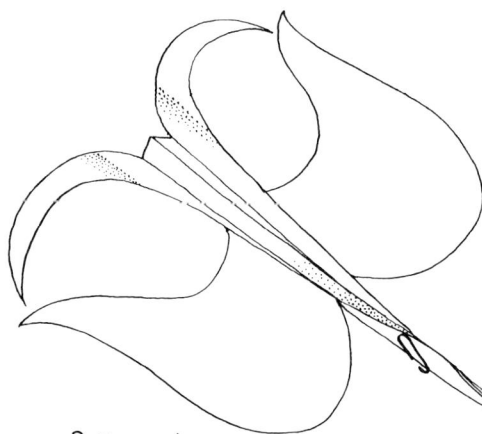

CUT

FOLD ON DOTTED LINES

Paper clip holds folded paper of body together, and also weights it to make bird glide properly. Place clip 5cm.(2in.) from tip of beak

Pattern wings with bright colours

Balsa gliding hawk

You need: a piece of Balsa wood 2 × 2 cm. ($\frac{3}{4}$ × $\frac{3}{4}$ in.) and about 28 cm. (11 in.) long; Balsa 2 mm. ($\frac{1}{16}$ in.) thick for the wings and tail.

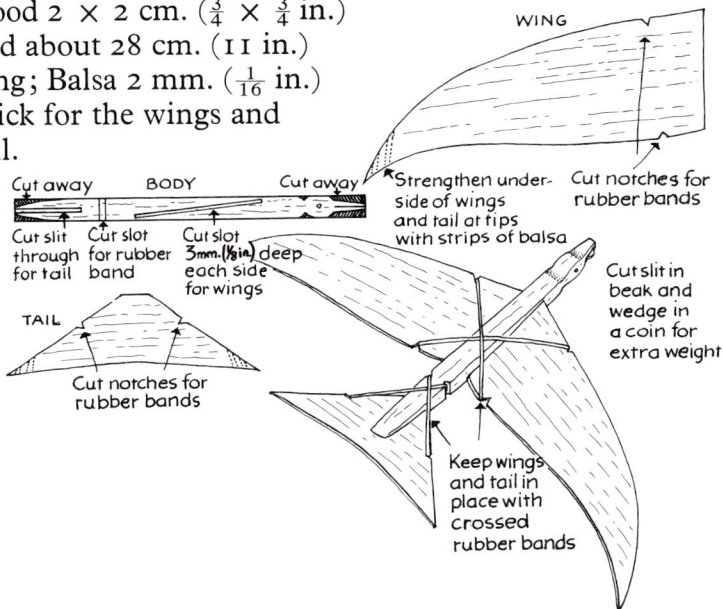

WING

Cut away   BODY   Cut away

Cut slit through for tail   Cut slot for rubber band   Cut slot 3mm.($\frac{1}{8}$in.) deep each side for wings

Strengthen under-side of wings and tail at tips with strips of balsa

Cut notches for rubber bands

Cut slit in beak and wedge in a coin for extra weight

TAIL

Cut notches for rubber bands

Keep wings and tail in place with crossed rubber bands

Large gliding flamingo

You need: Balsa 2 × 2 cm. ($\frac{3}{4}$ × $\frac{3}{4}$ in.) and about 60 cm. (2 ft.) long; a sheet of thin cardboard 50 × 63 cm. (20 × 25 in.)

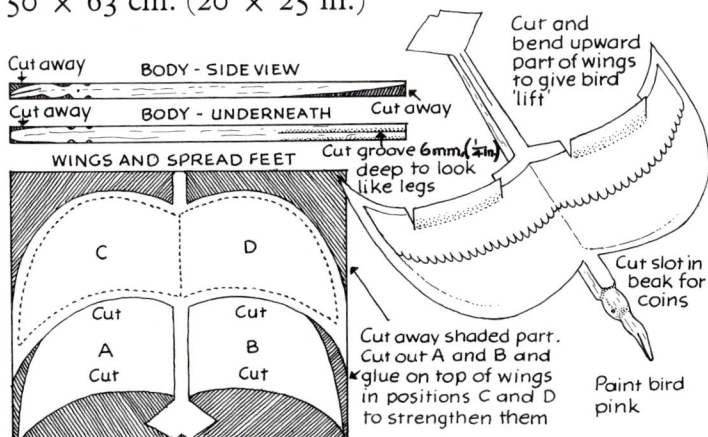

Cut away   BODY - SIDE VIEW

Cut away   BODY - UNDERNEATH   Cut away

WINGS AND SPREAD FEET

Cut groove 6mm.($\frac{1}{4}$in.) deep to look like legs

Cut and bend upward part of wings to give bird 'lift'

C   D

Cut   Cut

A   B

Cut   Cut

Cut slot in beak for coins

Cut away shaded part. Cut out A and B and glue on top of wings in positions C and D to strengthen them

Paint bird pink

Masks to make

(see p. 51)
Toucan
Cut out a cardboard mask
to fit your face. Cut slots at
a and **b** as shown. Cut a

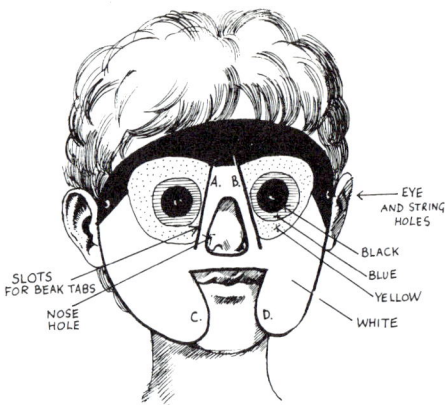

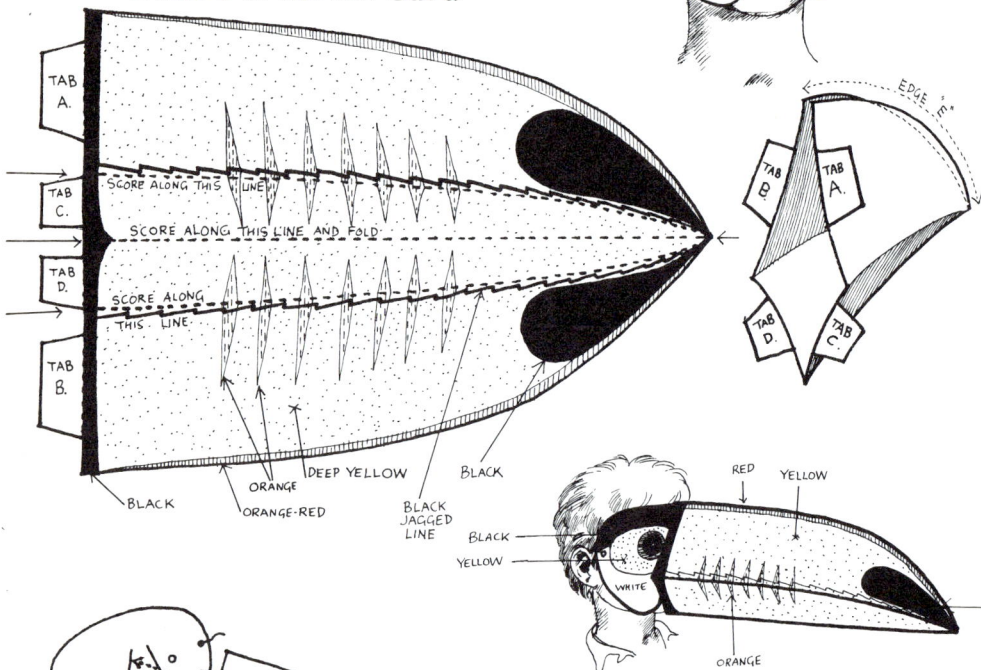

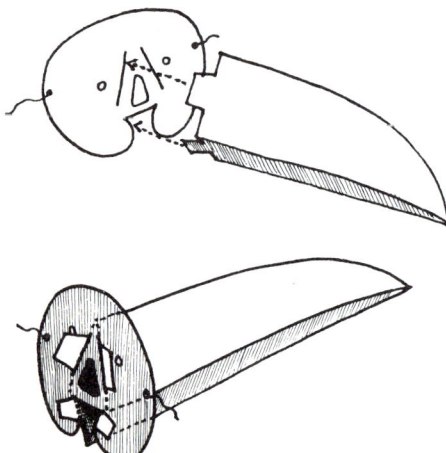

beak from a piece of card
45 × 30 cm. (18 × 12 in.)
as shown in the diagram.
Fold along the dotted lines
and glue along edge **e**.
Fit the tabs on the beak
through the slots in the
mask, bend them back and
glue them in place.

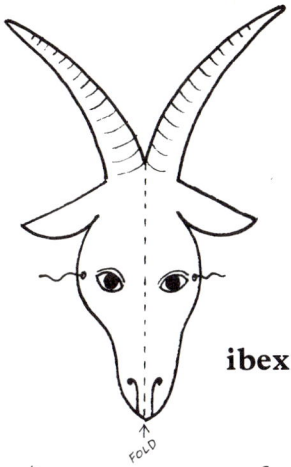

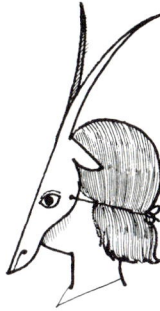

ibex

owl

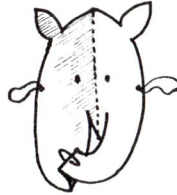

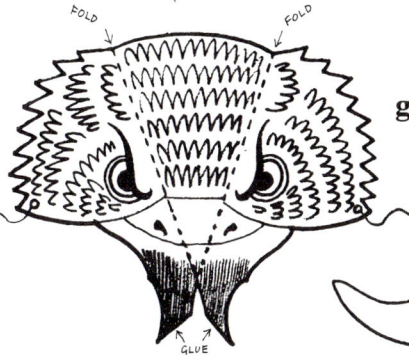

golden eagle

buffalo

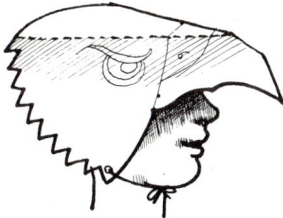

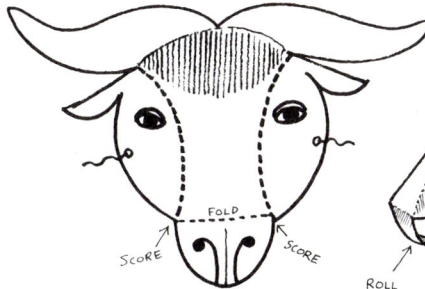

Each of these four simple masks is made from one piece of card folded along the dotted lines.

Clip back the bottom of the owl's face from inside with a paper clip so that the beak will stick out.

49

Wild boar
Cut out face, ears and tusks in card. Cut slots at **a** and **b**, wide slots at **c** and **d**, and make holes at **e** and **f**. Glue ears into slots **a** and **b** and the tusks at points marked **x**. Bend the mask into a cone shape and stick the edges together with sticky tape.

Queensland forest dragon
Cut the main shape from one piece of card. Glue a cardboard 'comb' to the top of the head and cut a ping-pong ball in half to use as eyes.

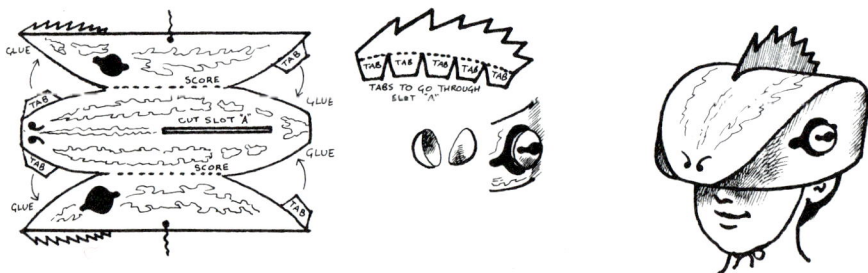

COMMON
MAGPIE
(Eurasia & N.America)

for
ANIMAL
ALPHABET

BLUE
MOCKING-
BIRD
(Mexico)

Design an animal alphabet

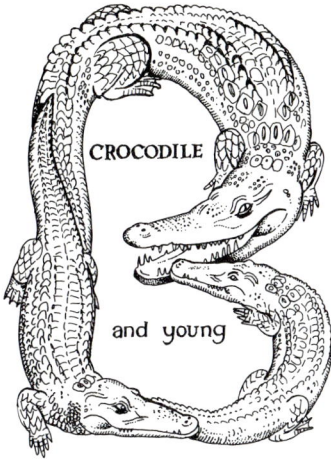

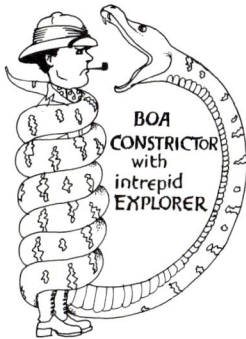

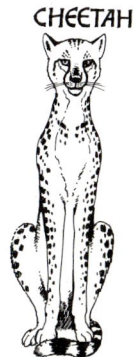

CROCODILE
and young

LEOPARD
attacking
ANTELOPE

BOA
CONSTRICTOR
with
intrepid
EXPLORER

CAT & DOG
waiting

STORK fishing

MONGOOSE
with
COBRA

CHEETAH

TWO BUCKING BRONCOS

MONKEY

SQUIRREL descending TREE

WOLF

VULTURES with old bones

GOAT eating leaves

HOUND chasing FOX

CAT with FISH

LIONESS pursuing STAG

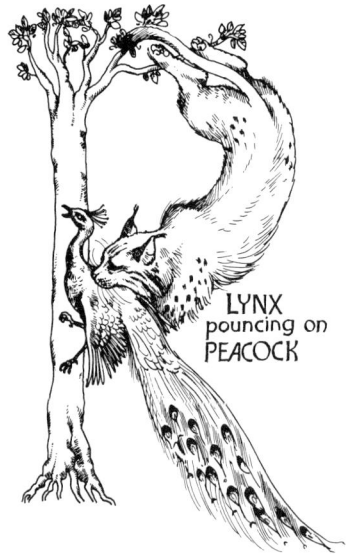

LYNX pouncing on PEACOCK

These are just suggestions for letters designed from animals. Try to think up your own ideas for designing your initials.

54

RATTLESNAKE

MOUNTAIN SHEEP

SHARK after Fish

GANNET

PELICAN with Fish

Two GIRAFFES

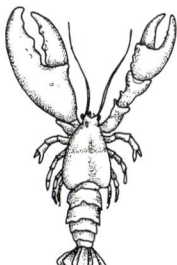

LOBSTER

TOUCAN

Animal skeletons

Monkey
You need: wire, white
drawing paper and glue.
Use a piece of wire 48 cm.
(19 in.) long for the body.
Twist onto it another
piece of wire 27 cm.
($10\frac{3}{4}$ in.) long at **y** to make
the other leg. Add a third
piece 60 cm ($23\frac{3}{4}$ in.) long
for the arms at **x**. Bend
to shape.

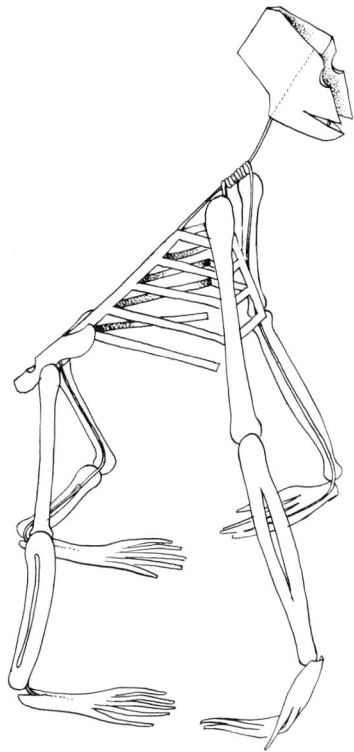

Head: Use a piece of paper
11 × 4.5 cm.
($4\frac{1}{4}$ × $1\frac{3}{4}$ in.). Crease it in
half and in half again. Fold
down the outside top ends
(diag. **2c**) and fold the
paper in half again. Trim
it to shape as in diagram
2d.

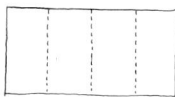
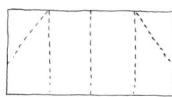
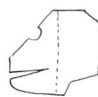

2a

2b

2c

2d

56

Ribs: You need paper 11 cm. ($4\frac{1}{4}$ in.) square. Make a crease down the middle, **3a**. Fold up the bottom corners, **3b**. Cut away the shaded areas in **3c**. Then open the paper out and cut away the spaces between the ribs, **3d**, using a sharp knife.

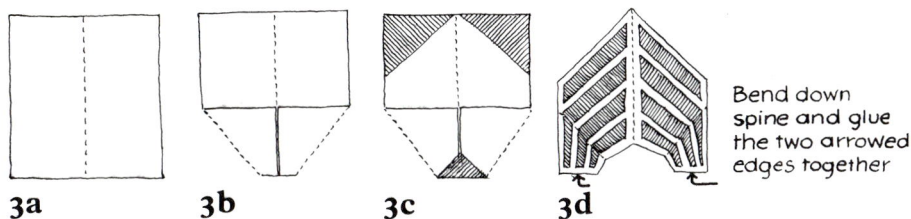

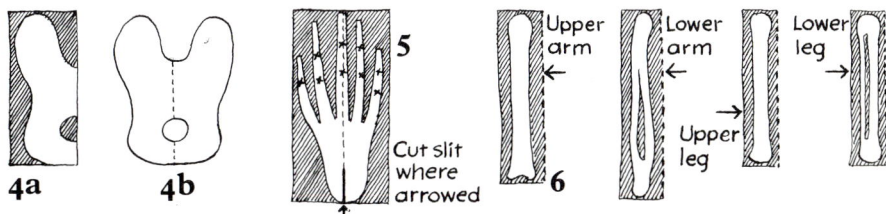

Bend down spine and glue the two arrowed edges together

3a   **3b**   **3c**   **3d**

4a   **4b**

5

Cut slit where arrowed

Upper arm

Lower arm

Lower leg

Upper leg

6

Hips: You need paper 5 × 4 cm. (2 × $1\frac{1}{2}$ in.). Fold it in half and cut away the shaded areas, **4a**.

Hands and feet: You need four pieces of paper about 6 × 3 cm. ($2\frac{1}{2}$ × $1\frac{1}{4}$ in.). Draw and cut out toes and fingers using diagram **5** as a guide.

Arms and legs: Cut out arm and leg bones as shown in diagram **6**, lengths as follows: upper arm 8 cm. ($3\frac{1}{4}$ in.), lower arm 10 cm. (4 in.), leg bones 7 cm. ($2\frac{3}{4}$ in).

Attach all paper bones to the wire with strong glue.

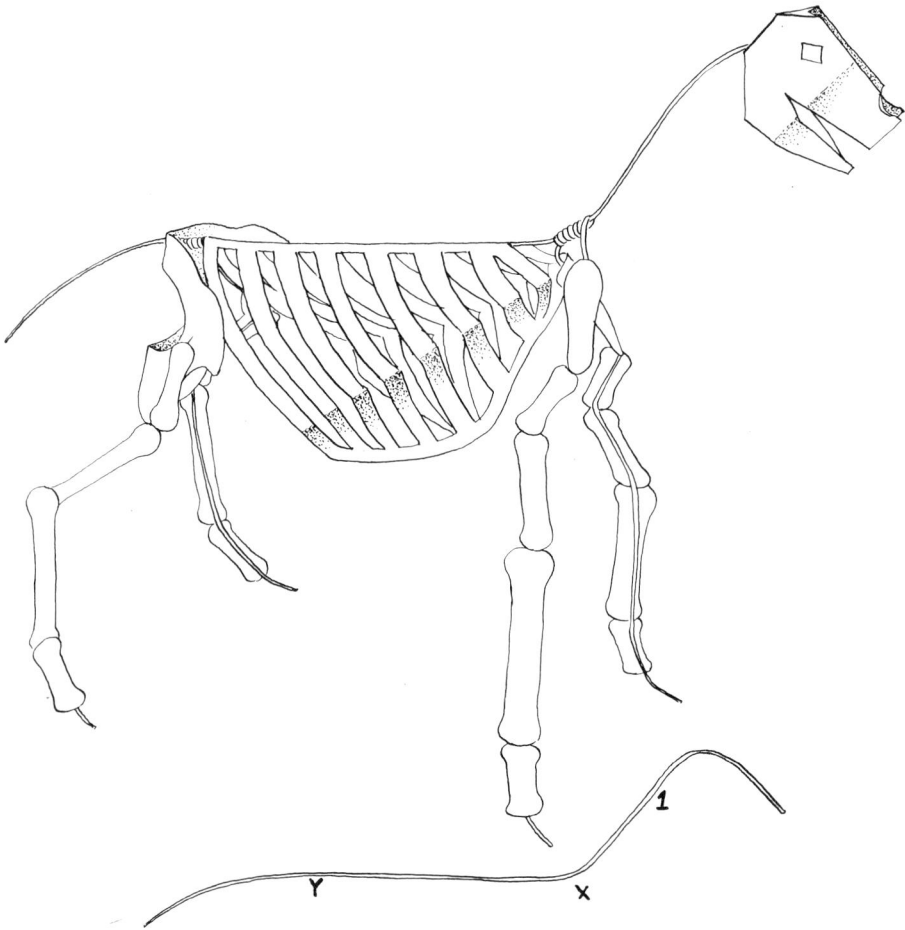

Quadruped (four-legged animal)

Cut a piece of wire 42 cm. (6½ in.) long for the body and bend it into shape, diagram **1**. Use wire 56 cm. (22 in.) long for the front legs. Bend it to shape (diag. **2**) and twist it onto the body at **x**. Use wire 51 cm. (20 in.) long for the back legs, bend them into shape (diag. **3**) and twist them onto the body at **y**.

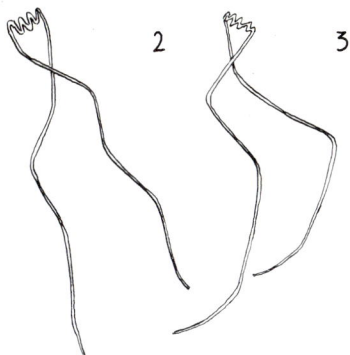

Head: You need a piece of paper 16.5 × 7 cm. (6½ × 2¾ in.). Make in the same way as for the monkey on page 56, following diagrams **4a-d**.

Ribs: You need paper 19 × 13 cm. (7½ × 5⅛ in). Follow diagrams **5a-d**.

4a

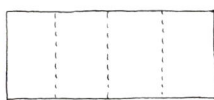

4b

4c

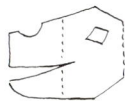

4d

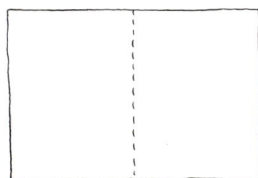

5a

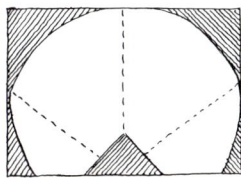

5c

6a

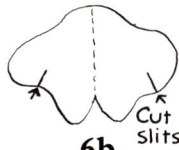

6b Cut slits

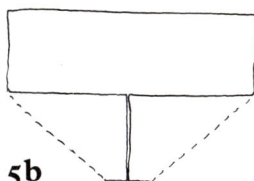

5b

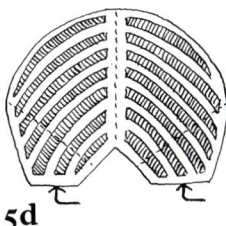

5d

Bend down spine and glue the two arrowed edges together

7

Hips: You need paper 13 × 7.5 cm. (5 × 3 in.). Follow diagrams **6a** and **b**.

Legs: Make several leg bones of the shape shown in diagram **7** and of several different sizes. Use the large quadruped picture to see how to fit them together. Fix the bones to the wire frame with strong glue.

The animal kingdom

On pages 62–63 you will find a chart of the animal kingdom, giving the scientific names of some of the main groups of creatures. (You will find these names used in natural history museums.) On the facing page are drawings of thirty-nine different creatures, each labelled with its popular name. Can you link each one with its scientific name? At the foot of page 63 are some clues indicating the natural home or habitat of the creatures shown. (Answers page 66)

Why not make your own giant-sized wall chart and cut out tiny animals to stick on it?

You could also make a quiz game of two sets of cards – one set with pictures of the animals on them and the other with the names of the groups and the habitat clues on them. Test how good your

ANTELOPE

ELEPHANT

TIGER

PARROTS

EAGLE

PLAICE

FLYING FISH

SALMON

HERRING

EEL

SQUIRREL

WHALE

MONKEY

KANGAROO

HEDGEHOG

PELICAN

ALBATROSS

CROCODILE

KING COBRA

GARPIKE

STURGEON

SHARK

PENGUINS

OSTRICH

TURTLE

FROG

HONEY BEE

BUTTERFLY

STAG BEETLE

WATER BUG

DRAGONFLY

JELLY FISH

SNAIL

OYSTER

EARTHWORM

STARFISH

SEA URCHIN

CRAB

SPIDER

friends are at matching up the pairs, and also how much
you have found out from this book about zoo animals.

The Animal Kingdom

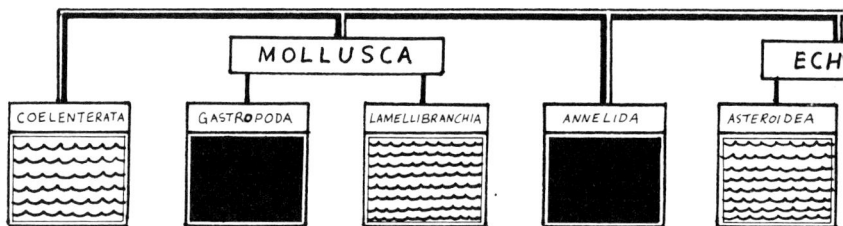

MOLLUSCA

ECH

| COELENTERATA | GASTROPODA | LAMELLIBRANCHIA | ANNELIDA | ASTEROIDEA |

VERTEBRATES

ANIMALS WITH BACKBONES
AMONG WHICH YOU FIND MAN.
ONLY 5% OF CREATURES ON
EARTH MAKE UP THE VERTEBRATES

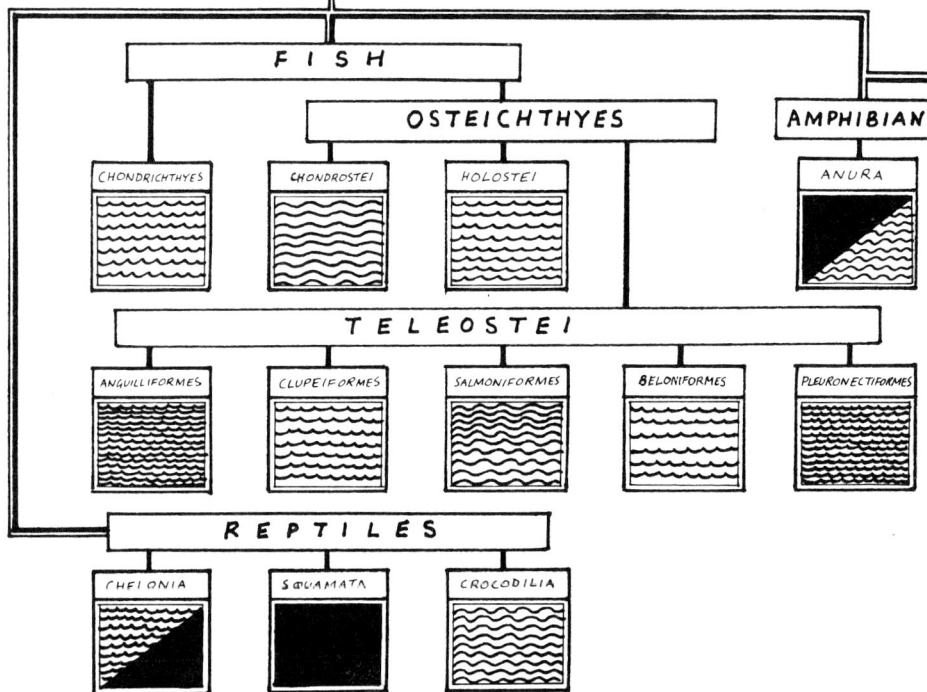

FISH

OSTEICHTHYES

AMPHIBIAN

| CHONDRICHTHYES | CHONDROSTEI | HOLOSTEI | ANURA |

TELEOSTEI

| ANGUILLIFORMES | CLUPEIFORMES | SALMONIFORMES | BELONIFORMES | PLEURONECTIFORMES |

REPTILES

| CHELONIA | SQUAMATA | CROCODILIA |

INVERTEBRATES

THESE ARE CREATURES WITHOUT BACKBONES. 95% OF THE ANIMAL KINGDOM CONSISTS OF INVERTEBRATES.

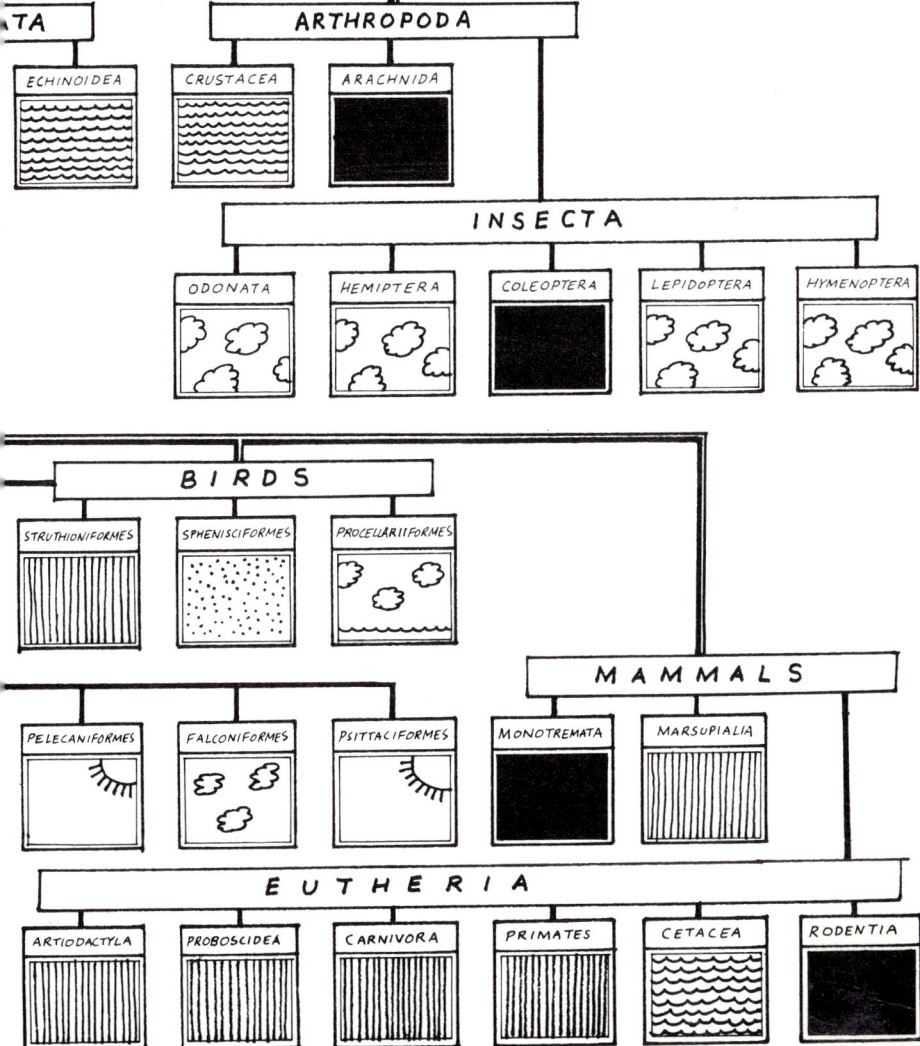

ARTHROPODA

...TA — ECHINOIDEA

CRUSTACEA — ARACHNIDA

INSECTA

ODONATA — HEMIPTERA — COLEOPTERA — LEPIDOPTERA — HYMENOPTERA

BIRDS

STRUTHIONIFORMES — SPHENISCIFORMES — PROCELLARIIFORMES

PELECANIFORMES — FALCONIFORMES — PSITTACIFORMES

MAMMALS

MONOTREMATA — MARSUPIALIA

EUTHERIA

ARTIODACTYLA — PROBOSCIDEA — CARNIVORA — PRIMATES — CETACEA — RODENTIA

CLUES

OCEANS

RIVERS

IN OR CLOSE TO THE GROUND

LAND CREATURE

COLD CLIMATE

AIRBORNE

AIRBORNE IN A HOT CLIMATE

AIRBORNE OVER SEA

63

Answers to quizzes

Page 7 Help! What is it?
Horns—greater kudu; face—giant panda; beak—golden eagle; forelegs and body—white rhino; back legs and tail—crocodile.

Page 11 Armour-plated animals
Did your list include an elephant and rhinoceros? It should have.

Pages 12 and 13 Feet and claws
armadillo has feet no. 19; black rhino 13; camel 20; crocodile 15; cheetah 14; eagle 8; elephant 5; frog 3; giant turtle 17; gorilla 18; kangaroo 7; lion 16; lizard 4; lobster 22; man 23; monkey 21; ostrich 1; parrot 12; platypus 11; polar bear 3; rabbit 10; roebuck 9; zebra 6.

Pages 14 and 15 Bills and beaks
The toucan has beak e; bullfinch c; great jacamar i; gannet h; bald eagle a; limpkin d; oropendola b; cockatoo f; ivory billed woodpecker h.

Insect-eating birds have slender pointed beaks, like the hedge sparrow, warbler or swallow.

Seed-eating birds have strong and wedge-shaped beaks, like the hawfinch, house sparrow or yellowhammer.

Fruit-eating birds have strong, long and sharp beaks, like the blackbird, song thrush or fieldfare.

Flesh-eating birds have hooked beaks, like the eagle, sparrow hawk or kestrel.

If you have thought of other examples, check your answers in an encyclopaedia.

Pages 16 and 17 Habitats
1 Inland waters: hippopotamus, flamingo, water buffalo, spoonbill, crocodile, pelican, shoebill.

2 Tropical forest: tiger, toucan, gibbon, leopard, loris, tapir, spotted linsang, orang-utan, okapi, silver pheasant.

3 Tropical grassland: lion, wildebeeste, giraffe, zebra, antelope, vulture, rhinoceros, cheetah, stork, waterbuck, baboon.

4 Coniferous forest: beaver, moose, brown bear, mink, long-eared owl, pine marten, lynx, blue hare.

5 Oceans and islands: gannet, albatross, boobie, komodo dragon, land rail, seal.

6 Desert: gecko, addax antelope, springbok, sand fox, stone curlew, water-storing tortoise.

7 Mountains: chamois, vicuna, yak, puma, alpine ibex, bighorn rams, mountain vulture, golden eagle.

Page 22 African animals
Apes are the species most closely related to man.
The hamadryas, chacma baboon, vervet monkey and gorilla
are all apes.

Page 23 American animals
Reptiles are cold-blooded animals with a scaly skin.
The rattlesnake, boa constrictor and iguana are all reptiles.

Page 28 Asian animals
The brown bear, mongoose, scorpion, Himalayan black bear and
pangolin all eat insects.

Page 28 Australian animals
The platypus and spiny anteater are both mammals which lay
eggs.

Pages 35–37 Animal characteristics
1 You could have said: water-loving (hippopotamus); tree-
climbing (marmoset); burrowing (cavey); flying (bat); plant-
eating (sloth); insect-eating (opossum).
2 A *hunting animal* combines great strength with great speed.
A *grazing animal* must eat all day because there is not much
goodness in the grass it eats. And that means it must have a large
stomach in which to store it all.
A *flesh-eater* has large sharp teeth for killing its prey and for
tearing the flesh of its victims.
Foraging animals have to be able to travel long distances looking
for food. They need long legs that will carry them anywhere and
long arms for reaching for food.
A *hunted animal* must be very fleet-footed and gifted with a very
keen sense of smell.
The very large eyes of *nocturnal animals* enable them to see at
night.
3 *hunting*—wolf; tiger, stoat
  grazing—horse, bison, deer
  flesh-eating—fox, leopard, cheetah
  foraging—chimpanzee, gorilla, orang-utan
  hunted—wildebeeste, impala, gazelle
  nocturnal—loris, lemur, linsang
4 The cheetah. It can run at 40 miles per hour.

Page 40 Patterned animals
The stripes are those of the tiger.
Deer and antelope are both white-bellied animals. The belly of
an animal is in shadow and generally looks very dark. A white
belly lessens this darkness so that it looks the same shade as the
animal's back. This means that the animal is less easily seen. It
is a form of camouflage.

Pages 42–44 Colour them correctly
Where do these birds live?
king penguin—Antarctica
mandarin duck—East Asia and Japan
yellow-headed Amazon parrot—Mexico, Ecuador, Brazil
rainbow lorikeet—East Indies and Australia
peafowl—India
jungle fowl—South-east Asia
blue-crowned pigeon—New Guinea
golden pheasant—China
black-capped lory—Ceram and Amboina Islands
golden conure—Brazil
kingfisher—Eurasia and Africa
scarlet macaw—Mexico and Bolivia
blue tit—Europe, Asia Minor
sulphur-breasted toucan—Mexico and Venezuela

Page 45 Animal crossword
Clues across: **1** dingo, **3** tern, **5** antelope, **6** wheatear, **10** bait,
11 tapir, **13** bee, **14** adders
Clues down: **1** drab, **2** owl, **3** tip, **4** newt, **6** whales, **7** eat, **8** eland,
9 grass, **12** cat

Pages 60–63 The animal kingdom

antelope—Artiodactyla	elephant—Proboscidea
tiger—Carnivora	parrot—Psittaciformes
eagle—Falconiformes	plaice—Pleuronectiformes
flying fish—Beloniformes	salmon—Salmoniformes
herring—Clupeiformes	eel—Anguilliformes
squirrel—Rodentia	whale—Cetacea
monkey—Primates	kangaroo—Marsupialia
hedgehog—Monotremata	pelican—Pelicaniformes
albatross—Procellariiformes	crocodile—Crocodilia
king cobra—Squamata	garpike—Holostei
sturgeon—Chondrostei	shark—Chondrichthyes
penguin—Sphenisciformes	ostrich—Struthioniformes
turtle—Chelonia	frog—Anura
honey bee—Hymenoptera	butterfly—Lepidoptera
stag beetle—Coleoptera	water bug—Hemiptera
dragonfly—Odonata	jellyfish—Coelenterata
snail—Gastropoda	oyster—Lamellibranchia
earthworm—Annelida	starfish—Asteroidea
sea urchin—Echinoidea	crab—Crustacea
spider—Arachnida	

Index

68